SOLUTIONS MANUAL
FOR

ENVIRONMENTAL ECONOMICS

Second Edition

CHARLES D. KOLSTAD

PREPARED BY

CHRISTOPHER C. GOODWIN
University of California Santa Barbara

&

EDMUND M. BALSDON
San Diego State University

Oxford University Press, Inc., publishes works that further Oxford University's objective of excellence in research, scholarship, and education.

Oxford New York
Auckland Cape Town Dar es Salaam Hong Kong Karachi
Kuala Lumpur Madrid Melbourne Mexico City Nairobi
New Delhi Shanghai Taipei Toronto

With offices in
Argentina Austria Brazil Chile Czech Republic France Greece
Guatemala Hungary Italy Japan Poland Portugal Singapore
South Korea Switzerland Thailand Turkey Ukraine Vietnam

For titles covered by Section 112 of the US Higher Education Opportunity Act, please visit www.oup.com/us.he for the latest information about pricing and alternate formats.

Published by Oxford University Press, Inc.
198 Madison Avenue, New York, New York 10016
http://www.oup.com

ISBN 978-0-19-975589-9

Printed in the United States of America
on acid-free paper

Contents

Chapter 2 Solutions

1. Individual answers may vary. Data for the example below was collected for the contiguous States of the U.S.A* (except CT, MA, NJ, and RI). Average farm market value per acre was obtained from the USDA 2002 Census of Agriculture as a proxy for agricultural profit. Average December temperature between 1971 and 2000 was obtained from the National Oceanic and Atmospheric Administration Earth System Research Laboratory.

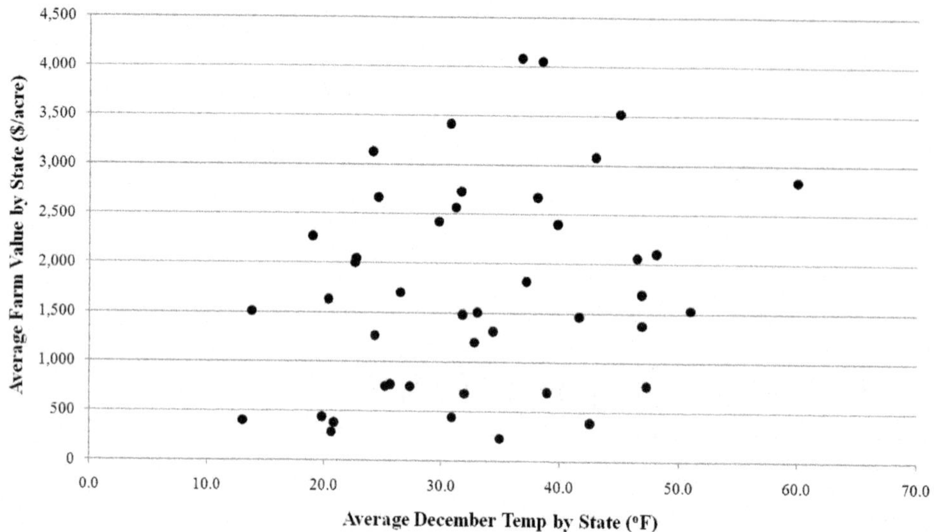

There appears to be a positive correlation between average December temperature and agricultural land value for States in the U.S.A. There are certainly other additional variables that would increase the explanatory power of this data. Other such variables might include soil characteristics, average precipitation, or proximity to an urban center - see Mendelsohn et al. (1994) for the explanatory variables used in their research. We might suppose that a 3°C increase in average annual temperature would result in an increase in agricultural land value in the U.S.A., ceteris parabis, based on the hypothesized positive correlation between average December temperature and agricultural land value.

*The data used in this answer was obtained in September 2010 from:
http://www.agcensus.usda.gov/Publications/2002/index.asp
http://www.esrl.noaa.gov/psd/data/usclimate/tmp.state.19712000.climo

2. a. We can proceed by replacing the parameters α, β, δ, and λ with the values given in the text and set each equation equal to 0:

$$\tfrac{dM}{dt} = 0.5E(t) - 0.005M(t) \overset{set}{=} 0 \quad \Rightarrow \quad E^* = 0.01M(t)$$

$$\tfrac{dT}{dt} = 0.02\big[0.003M(t) - T(t)\big] \overset{set}{=} 0 \quad \Rightarrow \quad T^* = 0.003M(t)$$

b. Given the assumption that steady-state World GDP is \$100 trillion we can convert the vertical axis of Figure 2.2 in the text from Percent Loss of GDP to Damage in dollar units.

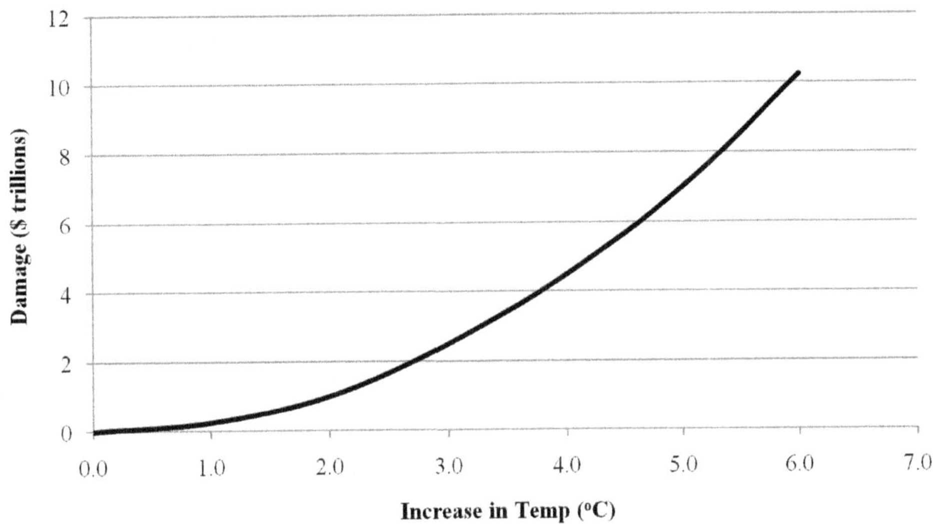

We can now take the average slope between two successive points on the x-axis graph to approximate the marginal damage at the midpoint of those two points, as shown in the figure below.

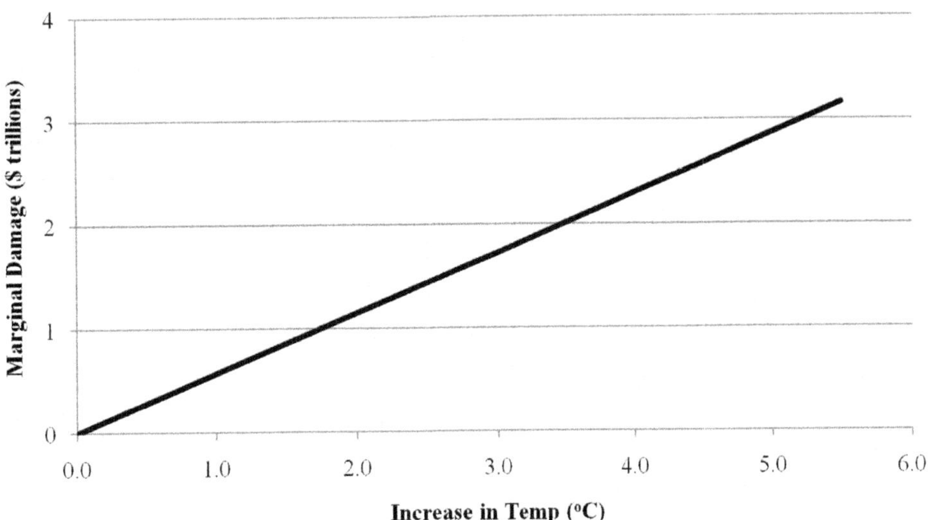

c. Given the assumption that the steady-state uncontrolled level of emissions is 12 billion tons of carbon, our marginal damage curve in part (b), and the two equations in part (a) we can create a plot, as below, showing the marginal damage ($ per ton of carbon emissions) as a function of the fraction of emissions controlled.

$$
\begin{aligned}
E^*(uncontrolled) = 12 = 0.01M(t) &\Rightarrow M^* = 1200 \\
&\Rightarrow T^* = 3.6 \\
&\Rightarrow MD(uncontrolled) \approx \$207/tCarbon \\
E^*(10\%\ controlled) = 10.8 = 0.01M(t) &\Rightarrow M^* = 1080 \\
&\Rightarrow T^* = 3.24 \\
&\Rightarrow MD(10\%\ controlled) \approx \$186/tCarbon \\
E^*(20\%\ control) = 9.6 = 0.01M(t) &\Rightarrow M^* = 960 \\
&\Rightarrow T^* = 2.88 \\
&\Rightarrow MD(20\%\ control) \approx \$165/tCarbon
\end{aligned}
$$

etc...

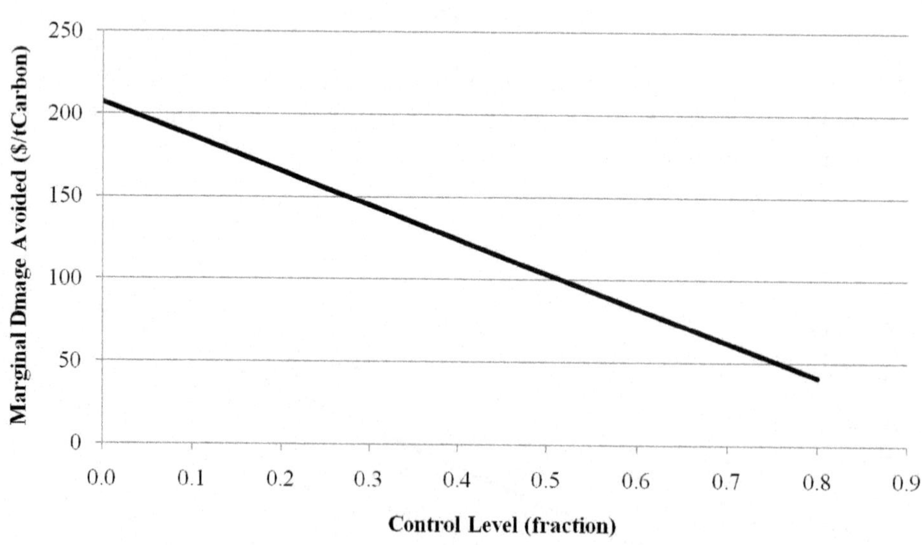

d. By combining or overlaying the graph in part (c) with Figure 2.3 in the text we can identify the optimal level of control as the intersection between the Marginal Damage Avoided curve and the Marginal Cost curve. It seems that these graphs show that the optimal level of carbon emissions control is about 40%.

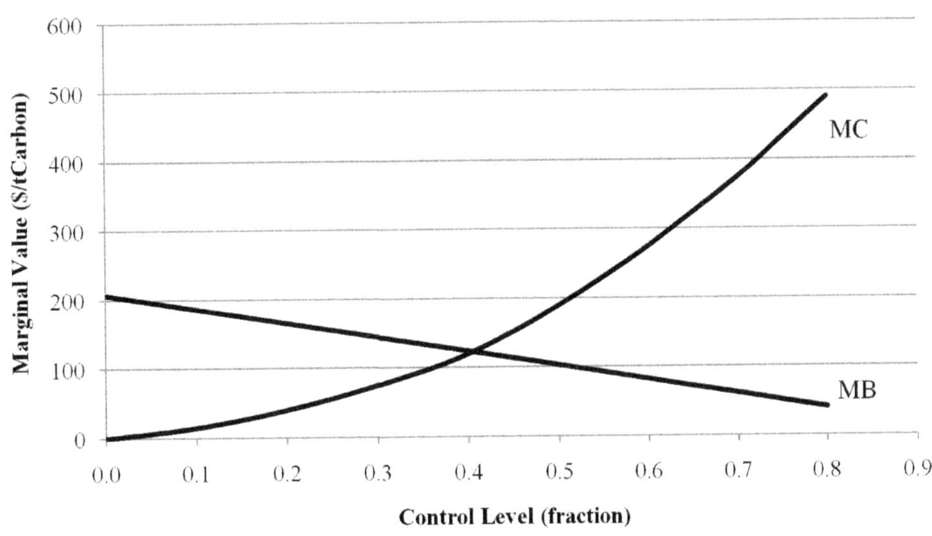
600
500
400
300
200
100
0
Marginal Value ($/tCarbon)
MC
MB
0.0
0.1
0.2
0.3
0.4
0.5
0.6
0.7
0.8
0.9
Control Level (fraction)

Chapter 3 Solutions

1. a. The Pareto criterion fails to satisfy A1: Completeness. Not all social alternatives can be compared using a Pareto-criterion framework. For example, two points on the Pareto frontier cannot be compared.

   b. Plurality-rule voting fails to satisfy A6: Independence of Irrelevant Alternatives. A counterexample, where the outcome of a two-way vote is altered by the inclusion of a third voting option, is easy to construct. See page 59 of the text for an example.

   c. Majority-rule voting fails to satisfy A5: Transitivity, as mentioned in the text and as demonstrated in Problem 5 from this chapter. Under some circumstances we may also imagine that majority-rule voting could also violate A1: Completeness if the vote between two choices is evenly split.

   d. Pulling a choice out of a hat (random) fails to satisfy A2: Unanimity and A6: Independence of Irrelevant Alternatives. The failure of A2: Unanimity seems obvious from the definition in the text. We can also see how the introduction of irrelevant alternatives in the hat will be likely to violate A6 with probability

   $$\text{P(A6 violated)} = \prod_{j=1}^{n+k} \frac{1}{j}$$

   where n is the number of alternatives originally in the hat and k is the number of alternatives added.

---

2. a. Plan A would be rejected compared to the status quo under the Pareto criterion. Plan B would also be rejected under the Pareto criterion.

   b. Plan A would be rejected compared to the status quo by a majority-rule vote, while Plan B would be accepted.

   c. Plan A and Plan B are both rejected compared to the status quo under the compensation principle. The fact that the cost of the "smoke guzzler" is more than the total willingness to pay for every person on the island indicates that there is no way of dividing the cost such that everyone could be made better off.

---

3. "Taxing each person equally" means a \$2 tax for every resident. A vote on this proposition would fail to gain a majority, since 60% of the population is willing to pay only \$1 to reduce pollution, and would therefore be expected to vote against it. By the same logic, this proposition as it stands is not a Pareto improvement: the 60% would be made worse off by paying \$2 for pollution control when their willingness to pay is only \$1.

   The proposal is desirable, however, using the compensation principle. The 40% willing to pay \$100 could compensate the 60% sufficiently to gain their support. \$1 to each of these 600,000 residents requires \$600,000. The other 400,000 residents have a surplus of $(100 - 2) \cdot 400,000 = \$39,200,000$. That is, we should say they could *easily* compensate the 60%. The compensation principle states that this proposition is desirable because this possibility exists, even if the compensation doesn't actually take place.

Economists defend using the compensation principle based on the following intuition: If the sum of willingnesses to pay for a project in society is greater than the cost of that project, then it should be undertaken. In this sense, the principle separates the desirability of a project from its proposed financing. For instance, a plan to finance the project described by charging one randomly chosen resident all $2,000,000 is also desirable based on the compensation principle.

---

4. Only points Z and R are Pareto preferred to point W. All the other points are not comparable to W under the Pareto criterion.

---

5. The rankings given in the problem are:

	Boris	Maggie	William
First	H	D	K
Second	K	H	D
Third	D	K	H

In a vote between two alternatives, each person simply votes for the activity he/she ranks higher. The format is that two activities are paired for a vote, then the winner is paired with the third. For instance:

H vs. $K \longrightarrow H$ wins

H vs. $D \longrightarrow D$ wins

But what happens if D, the apparent winner, is paired with K, the first activity eliminated?

D vs. $K \longrightarrow K$ wins

We see that the outcome, the Condorcet winner, of this two-step process depends on the order of the pairings. Continuing to match the winner with the third-place activity leads to cyclical rounds of voting.

---

6. The utility function from the problem is

$$U(x, H) = x + H - 1/x - 1/H$$

where $H_t = H_{t-1} + g(100 - H_{t-1}) - nx$.

a. This is really not a framework consistent with biocentrism. An implication here is that value is derived from utility enjoyed by humans; there is no consideration for intrinsic value. A biocentrist would have a different type of objective function, one based on the intrinsic value of living things, of which human utility would be only a part. The fact that the above utility function depends directly on x is sufficient to invalidate it as biocentric. A biocentric objective function would be more likely to depend only on H.

This is essentially an anthropocentric utility function, but it is important to emphasize that the current framework allows for indirect sources of utility. The H argument in the function above is meant to include the traditional anthropocentric form of instrumental value, but also indirect value derived by people from H. This can include value as intangible as knowledge of the existence of natural environments never seen first hand.

b. $H = 100$ implies the environment begins at the pristine level. Consumption of x at the three levels reduces H, and a steady state level of H is reached for each. By evaluating this question in a spreadsheet we can see that the higher the level of x, the lower is the steady-state level of H.

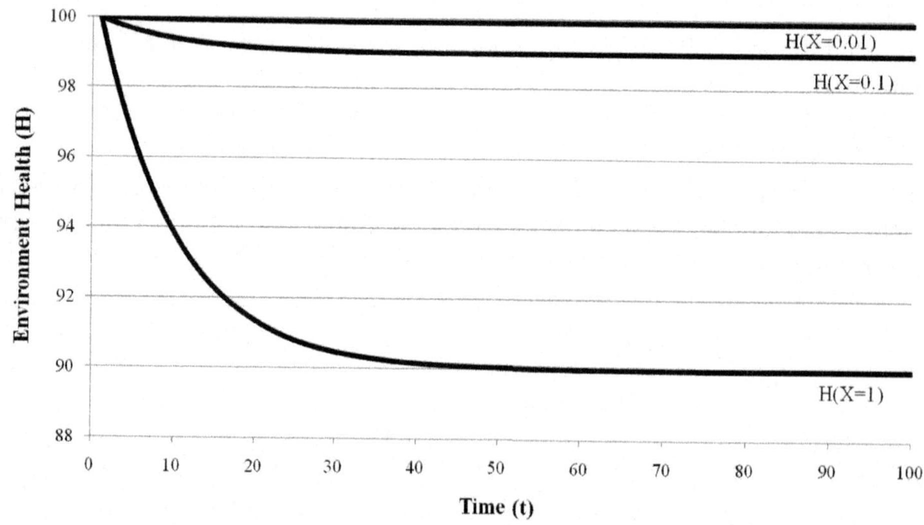

c. Plotting the Utility for this single person (recall $n = 1$) through time we obtain the following results for the three different levels of consumption x.

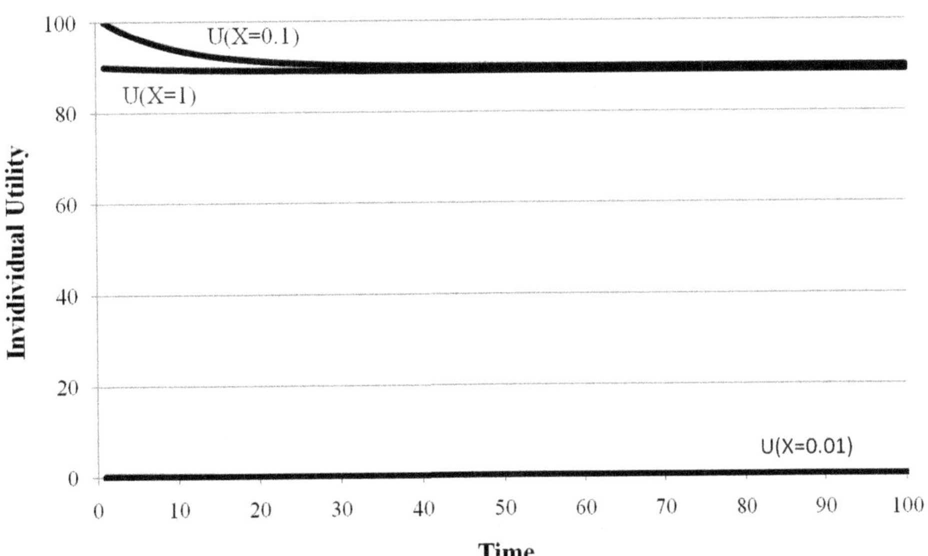

By trying differing levels of x we find that $x = \frac{3}{10}$ maximizes the total utility for this single person economy.

---

7. The following table lists the bundles in order of preference for Tucker and Finch:

	Tucker		Finch	
	Food	Sport	Food	Sport
First	2.1	1.0	1.4	1.4
Second	1.0	2.0	1.0	2.0
Third	2.4	0.7	1.6	1.3
Fourth	1.7	1.3	1.8	1.1
Fifth	2.0	1.0	2.0	1.0

a. Plotting these bundles for each person we can draw our hypothesized indifference curves that pass through the point (1.0, 2.0) as in the figure below. Answers may vary on the shape of these curves - any curve through the (1.0, 2.0) point that is below the first point and above the third through fifth points is sufficient. Remember that the indifference curve should not drop below 0.9 units of Sport for Tucker or 1.2 units of Sport for Finch.

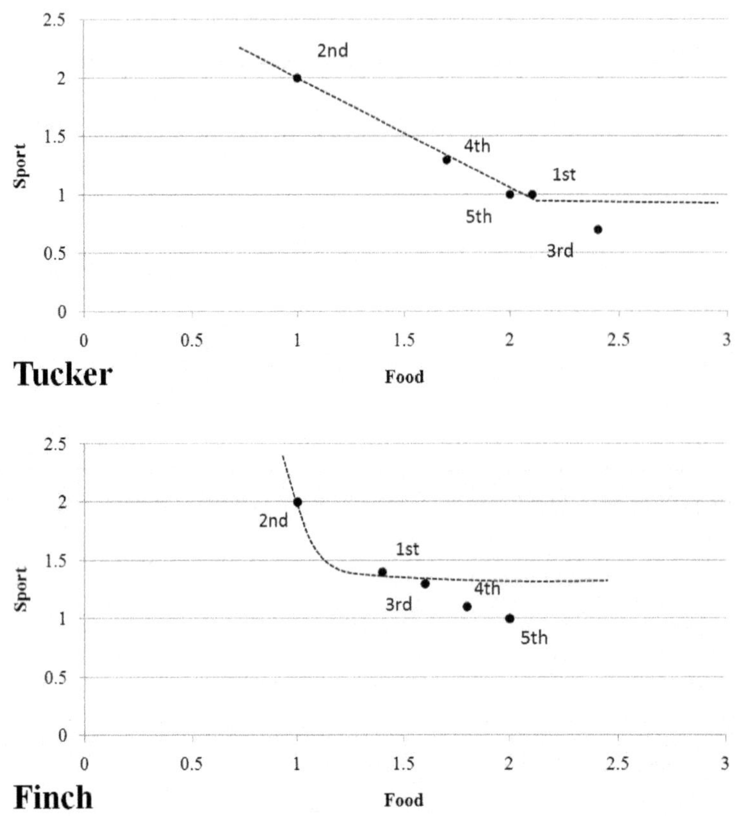

b. Using the preference relationships given we see for Tucker: C ► B ► A, and for Finch: C ► B ► A. We conclude that between choice A and B, society would prefer choice B since choice B results in the attainment of a higher indifference curve for both Tucker and Finch than does choice A.

c. By summing up the total amount of Food and Sport from social choice A we see that we have 4.0 units of food and 2.0 units of sport. From this total amount we could allocate the bundle (2.4, 0.7) to Tucker, and the bundle (1.6, 1.3) to Finch. We see that this new allocation from social choice A would be prefered to social choice B, and thus we have reversed the social choice preference in part (b).

d. The result in part (c) suggests there is a flaw in the compensation principle since neither Tucker nor Finch prefer A to B without the redistribution outlined in part (c).

8. Following the suggestion in the text we define the following preference relationship for 3 people (1-3) and 3 choices (X-Z).

Person	Preference
1	X ▶ Y ▶ Z
2	Y ▶ Z ▶ X
3	X ▶ Z ▶ Y

Using the Borda Count methodology we see that choice X has a score of 5, choice Y has a score of 6, and choice Z has a score of 7.

We now include choice W with the following ordered preference relationships for each person (while still preserving the original preference relationships between choices X, Y, and Z.

Person	Preference
1	X ▶ Y ▶ Z ▶ W
2	Y ▶ Z ▶ W ▶ X
3	X ▶ Z ▶ Y ▶ W

Under the Borda Count system choice X now has a score of 6, Y has a score of 6, Z has a score of 7, and W has a score of 11. Choice X and choice Y are now tied for first place. Clearly, choice W was not an irrelevant alternative - it placed last by the Borda count but it affected the social choice outcome.

---

9. We can set up the preference relationship between choices A, B, and C for person 1, 2, and 3 as follows:

Person	Preference
1	A ▶ B ▶ C
2	B ▶ C ▶ A
3	C ▶ A ▶ B

In pairwise majority-rule voting we have the following combinations and outcomes:

A vs. B $\longrightarrow$ A wins

B vs. C $\longrightarrow$ B wins

C vs. A $\longrightarrow$ C wins

This example shows how pairwise majority voting can violate axiom A5 Transitivity.

---

10. We state the preference relationship between choices A, B, and C for persons 1 through 5 as follows:

Person	Preference
1	A ▶ B ▶ C
2	A ▶ B ▶ C
3	C ▶ B ▶ A
4	C ▶ B ▶ A
5	B ▶ C ▶ A

In the first round of runoff voting choice C is eliminated, in the second round choice A is eliminated leaving choice C the winning outcome of the social choice mechanism. Using the instant runoff voting mechanism the social outcome ordering is C ▶ A ▶ B . If, however, choice A is dropped as an irrelevant alternative and the social choice mechanism is re-run, we find that the social choice ordering of C and B changes such that B ▶ C – a clear violation of axiom A6: Independence of irrelevant alternatives.

Chapter 4 Solutions

1. a. The profit maximizing firms in the perfectly competitive market each set marginal revenue equal to marginal cost, where each of their marginal revenue curves are MR = P. As represented by point A on the figure below: $q^*_{comp} = 40$ and $p^*_{comp} = 10$.

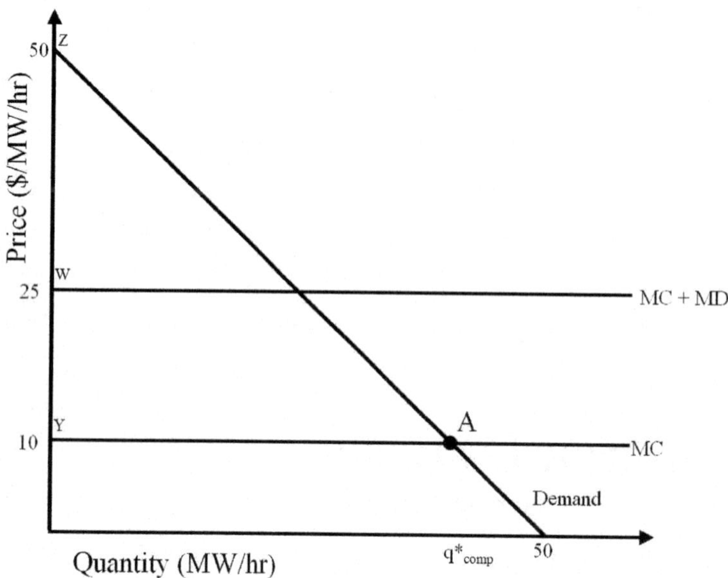

b. The monopolist sets marginal revenue to marginal cost, where their marginal revenue is MR = 50 − 2*Q*. Thus, as represented by point B in the figure below, $q^*_{mon} = 20$ and $p^*_{mon} = 30$.

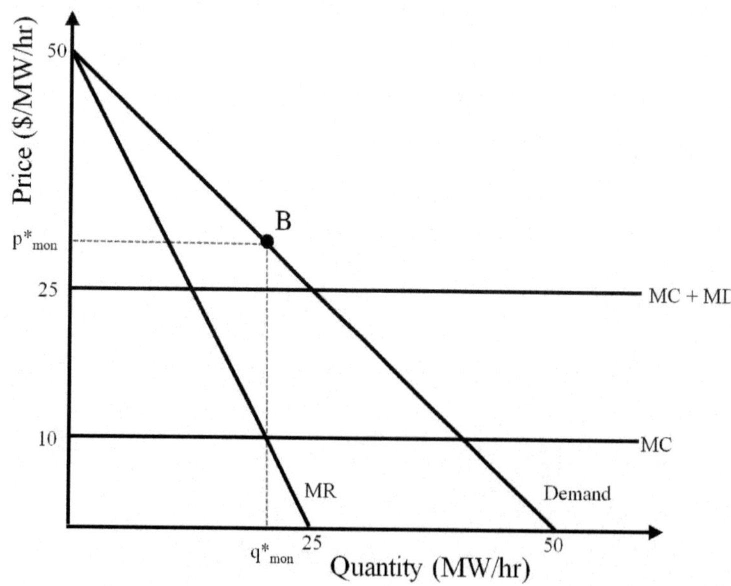

c. i. The net surplus is 200. As presented in the figure below, the net surplus in part (a) of the question is the sum of consumer surplus (CS) and producer surplus (PS) minus the pollution damage (Dmg).

CS = Area(AYZ) = $\frac{1}{2} \cdot 40 \cdot 40 = 800$
PS = Area(AY) = 0
Dmg = Area(AWXY) = $15 \cdot 40 = 600$

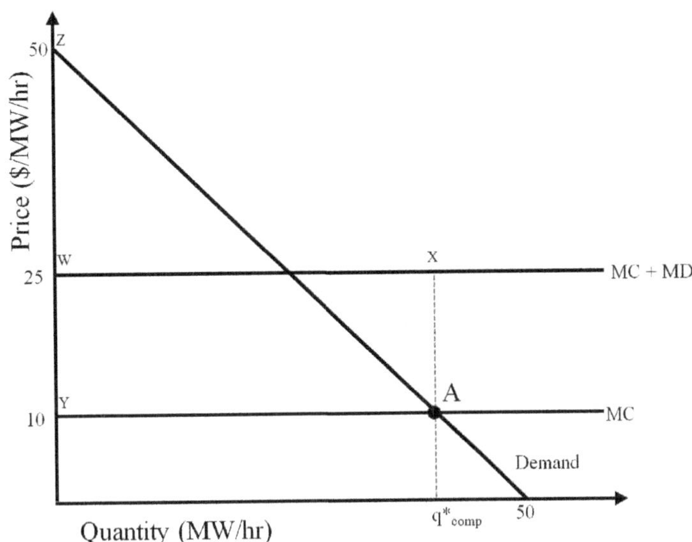

ii. The net surplus is 300. As presented in the figure below, the net surplus in part (b) of the question is the sum of the consumer surplus and the monopolist producer surplus minus the pollution damage Dmg.

CS = Area(BTZ) = $\frac{1}{2} \cdot 20 \cdot 20 = 200$
PS = Area(BTVY) = $20 \cdot 20 = 400$
Dmg = Area(UVWY) = $15 \cdot 20 = 300$

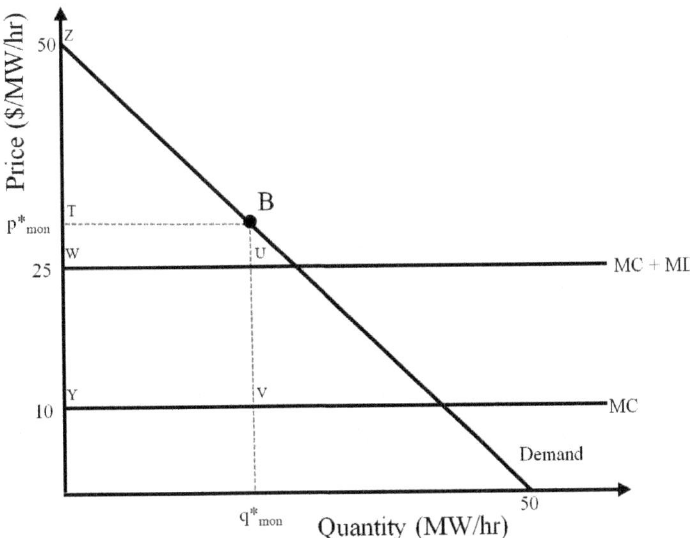

2. a. Point D in the figure below

   b. Point E in the figure below

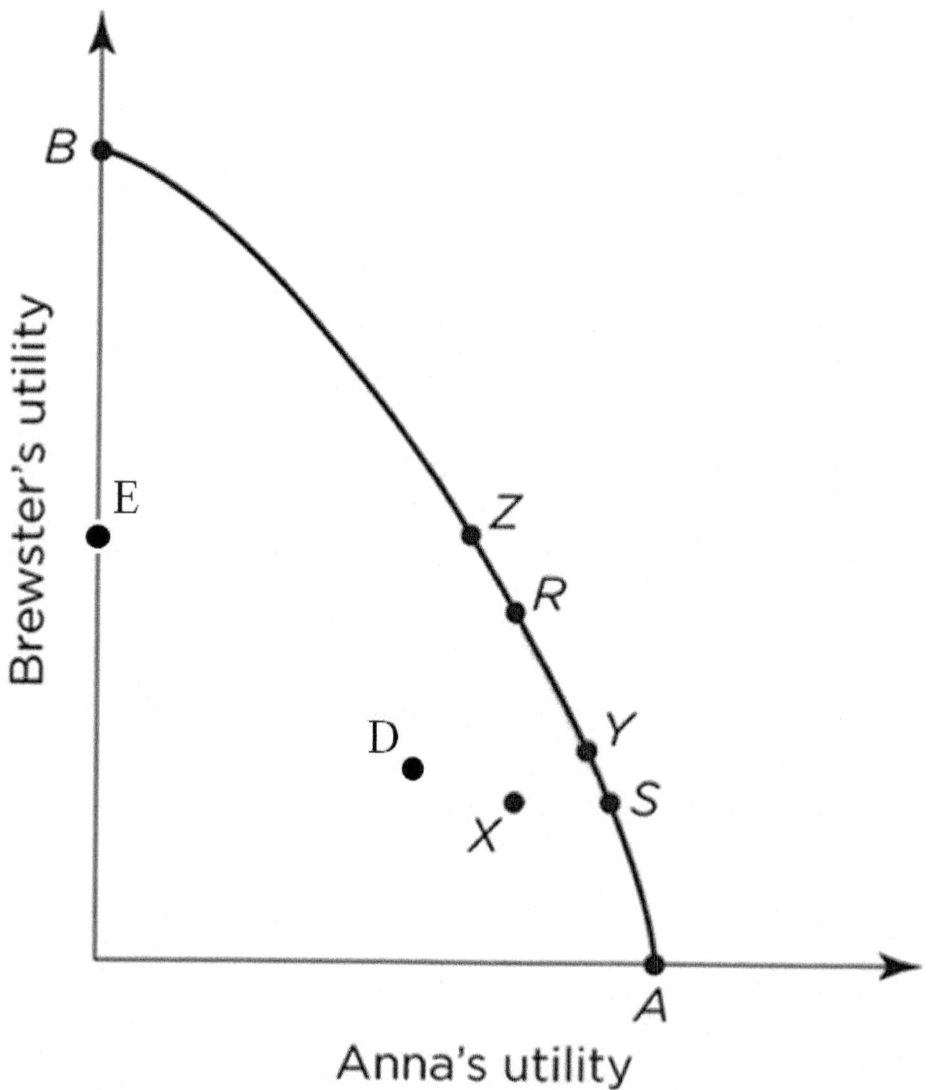

3. It seems completely reasonable that the MRT should get steeper as the economy produces less garbage disposal if the production of garbage disposal (and wine for that matter) is subject to diminishing marginal returns.

4. The amount of garbage disposal and wine is shown as q^*_G and q^*_W, respectively, on the figure below. These values are given by the point of tangency between Brewsters highest indifference curve and the production possibilites frontier. The slope at this point of tangency represents the reletive price ratio of the two goods.

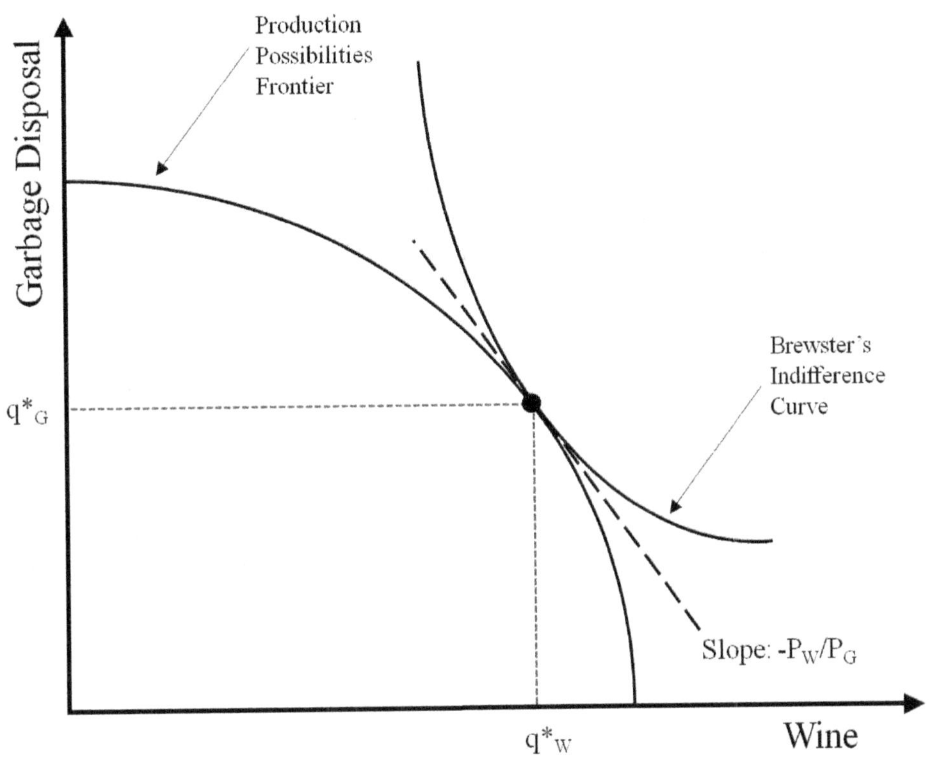

5. If ILS has an MRT of 2:1 then they would take 2 bags of garbage in exchange for the price of 1 bottle of wine. We are told that Brewster would be indifferent between giving up 1 bottle of wine and not getting rid of 3 bags of garbage. Thus Brewster would be willing to give up the price of 1 bottle of wine if ILS took 3 or more bags of garbage off his hands - but ILS would only take 2 or less bags of garbage in exchange for 1 bottle of wine. It seems that there is too much garbage disposal and we might expect that Brewster would be willing to retain more of his garbage and thus keep some more of the wine he gave up.

6. The text introduces in this chapter what will be called the *equimarginal principle* in subsequent chapters. It is argued that if there are many firms producing a good and a bad (in the text the example is wine and garbage, the more general example is any manufactured good and pollution), efficiency would require that the marginal rates of transformation be the same for each firm. That is to say that the production of one more unit of the good from any firm would result in the same amount of additional pollution. The logic goes that if this were not the case, the high-MRT firm (lots of pollution associated with each additional unit of output) could reduce output by one unit, while the low-MRT firm (less pollution from each additional unit of output) could increase output by one unit: Total output would remain the same, while total pollution would decrease, which is clearly the more efficient outcome. The existence of this potential Pareto improvement suggests that the initial allocation was inefficient. A potential Pareto improvement of this type is always possible unless the MRTs of all firms are the same.

   A more natural way of expressing this concept is in terms of pollution control costs. The marginal cost to a firm of controlling pollution is really its MRT: What the firm gives up to reduce pollution by an additional unit. A regulation that requires pollution reductions of 50% of emissions by all firms would reduce total pollution by 50%, but would it do so efficiently? Where firms have different control costs, the answer is no. By the logic outlined in the previous paragraph, a reallocation of pollution control activity toward the firms with lower marginal costs would produce a potential Pareto improvement.

7. The figure below depicts an Edgeworth Box with indifference curves for Humphrey and Matilda. First consider Humphrey: his utility depends on packs of cigarettes (a good) and rental payments (a bad). He therefore has upward sloping indifference curves of the type introduced in this chapter of the text. Their concave (downward) shape suggests diminishing marginal utility of smoking. Matilda's utility depends on *her* rental payments and *Humphrey's* smoking, both bads. As suggested by the hint in the problem, we can redefine the leftward direction on the horizontal axis for Matilda as smoke reduction (a good - for Matilda). Consider the interpretation of the upper-left and bottom-right corners of the box. Point C represents an arrangement where Humphrey pays 100% of the rent and smokes zero packs of cigarettes. This is the point of highest utility in the box for Matilda, and the point of lowest utility in the box for Humphrey. Point D is the opposite: Matilda pays all the rent and Humphrey smokes 20 packs of cigarettes. This is the feasible point of highest utility for Humphrey and lowest utility for Matilda.

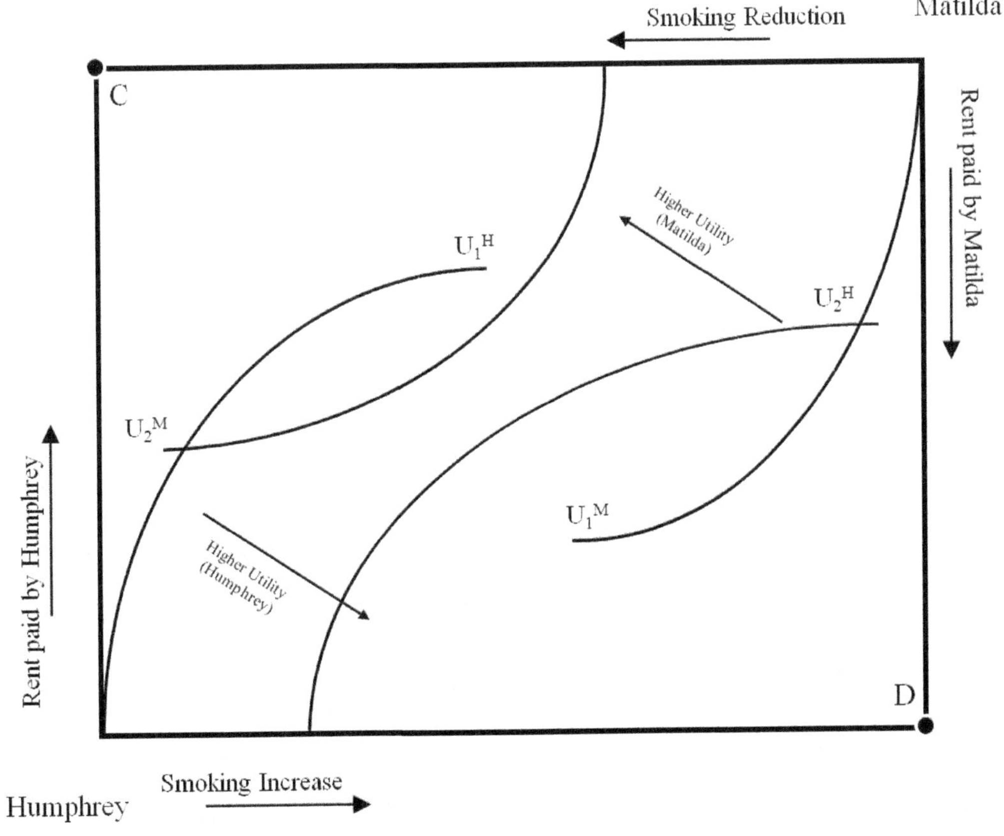

The two endowment points considered in the problem are labeled A and B inthe figure below. At point A, rent is split 50:50 and Humphrey smokes 20 packs per month. Indifference curves that pass through A are labeled U_M^A and U_H^A for Matilda and Humphrey, respectively. These indifference curves are not tangent to one another, suggesting that bargaining over rent and Humphrey's smoking can lead to a Pareto improvement. More specifically, consider the lens-shaped area to the south-west of A. All points inside the lens are preferred to A by both agents; it appears Matilda will be able to "buy down" Humphrey's smoking in an arrangement that makes both of them better off.

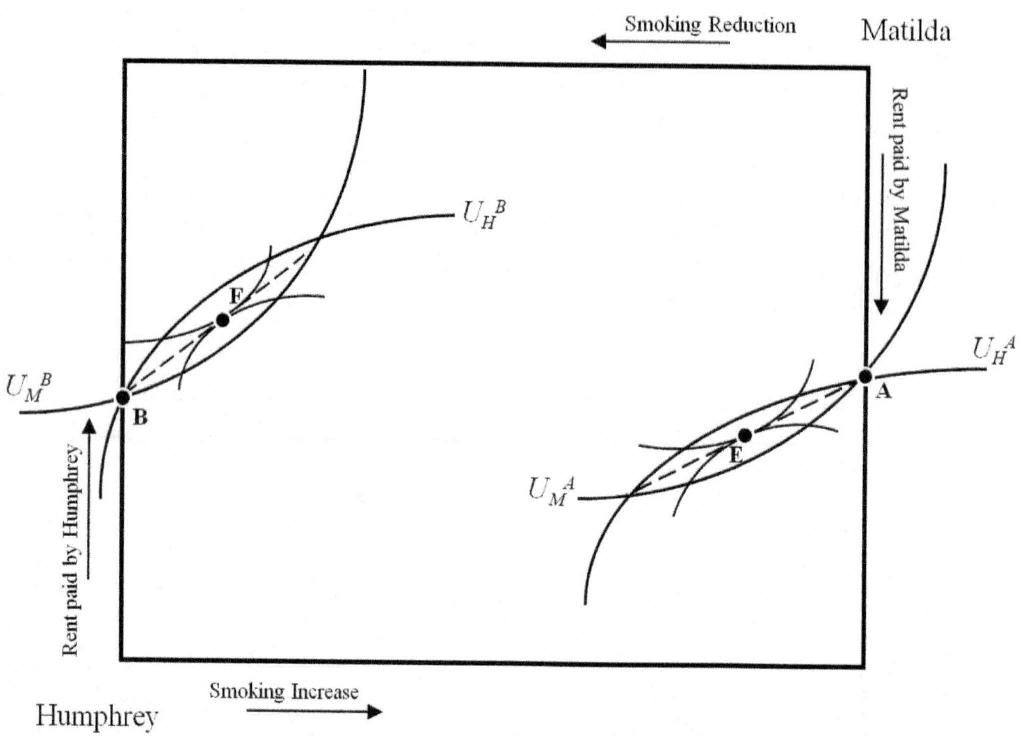

Bargaining would result in an allocation like point E. At E, their indifference curves are tangent, and no further mutually beneficial trades are possible. At E, the prevailing price of smoke reduction is reflected in the slope of the dashed line connecting points E and A. This is the rate at which Matilda must buy down her roommate's smoking.

Point B in the second figure represents the initial allocation where the rent is split 50:50, but a no-smoking arrangement is in place. Here the lens-shaped area of preferred allocations lies to the north-east, suggesting that bargaining will involve Humphrey paying Matilda for the right to smoke. An equilibrium arrangement would be supported by a point like F in the figure. Humphrey could pay his roommate a price per pack given by the slope of the dashed line that connects points B and F.

Notice that while the first arrangement would be strongly preferred by Humphrey, and the second strongly preferred by Matilda, both lead through bargaining to allocations that are Pareto optimal. This is the important result regarding the assignment of property rights to which the text returns in Chapter 13.

Chapter 5 Solutions

1. a. Huck and Matilda's demand curves (D_H, D_M) are presented in the figure below along with the aggregate demand (D_{Aggr}). We can characterize the inverse aggregate demand function as

$$P_{Aggr} = \begin{cases} 2 - 1\frac{1}{2}Q_{Aggr} & Q_{Aggr} \in [0,1) \\ 1 - \frac{1}{2}Q_{Aggr} & Q_{Aggr} \in [1,2] \end{cases}$$

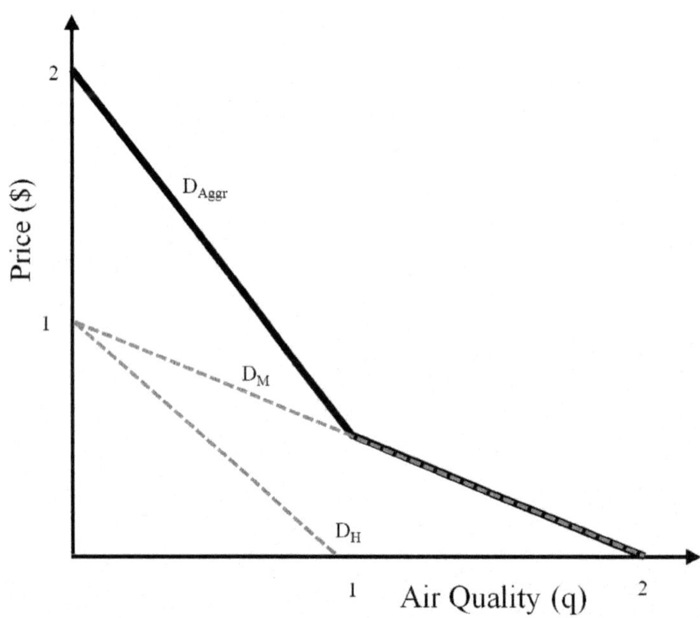

b. The efficient quantity of air quality is 0.8 and is found where Supply $\stackrel{set}{=}$ Aggregate Demand as seen in the figure below. In this case, $Q \stackrel{set}{=} 2 - 1\frac{1}{2}Q_{Aggr}$.

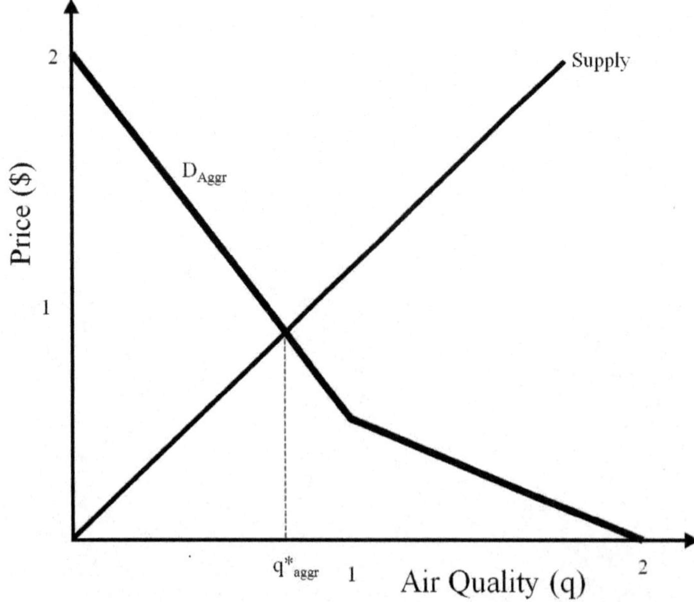

2. a. We are given that "noise costs" are $N = \frac{1}{d^2}$ and transportation costs are $T = 2d$ (\$1 per kilometer, each way). Daily total costs are therefore given by

$$\text{Daily TC} = \text{T+N} = \frac{1}{d^2} + 2d$$

b. Where would Fritz live? He will choose d to minimize total costs from noise and transportation. Differentiating TC with respect to d and setting this expression equal to zero, the condition for minimization of the function in part (a) is

$$\frac{\partial TC}{\partial d} = -\frac{2}{d^3} + 2 \overset{set}{=} 0 \quad \Rightarrow d^3 = 1 \quad \Rightarrow d^* = 1 \text{ km}$$

Daily total costs are minimized where $d = 1$ km and Fritz's total cost is 3.

c. Fritz is now told he will be compensated for any noise damage he suffers. Total costs are now given by

$$\text{TC} = 2d + \frac{1}{d^2} - \frac{1}{d^2} = 2d$$

The problem is therefore reduced to one of minimizing travel costs. Fritz would move as close as possible to the airport, which in this case is $d = 0.1$ km. Compensation, in turn, is *maximized* at

$$\text{Compensation} = \text{N} = \frac{1}{d^2} = \frac{1}{(0.1)^2} = \$100$$

This outcome demonstrates what is known as "moving to the nuisance," and represents a strong argument against compensation based on damages for victims of externalities.

---

3. The concept of rivalry is sometimes called "depletability," since a nonrival good (or bad) is one for which consumption by one person does not *deplete* the stock of the good (bad) for others' consumption. The text has argued that pollution generally fits this formula: one urban dweller's exposure to air pollution does not reduce the amount of air pollution left over the city for others to "consume." However, the case of sulfur dioxide does not really fit. Once some of it falls to the ground and contaminates a given piece of land, it has been taken out of the air and cannot go elsewhere. In this sense it is a rival bad.

The Freeman paper cited in the hint goes on to suggest that acid deposition is nevertheless a public bad, since the recipients have no control over how much they receive. That is, nonexcludability can be sufficient to make a bad public.

---

4. Compensation is distortionary for the same reasons that taxes or subsidies are: because they affect the marginal decisions of consumers or firms, diverting behavior away from cost minimization. In problem 2 above, for instance, the compensation was based on damages from noise. As a result, the consumer's problem of choosing where to locate was eliminated of noise costs, and the new solution no longer represented a minimization of total costs.

Where taxes, subsidies, or compensation is levied *lump sum*, however, the marginal decisions are not altered. In problem 2 if the government had instead offered Fritz daily compensation of $2, but specified that this was independent of his location, his minimization problem would be unchanged. This would be a non-distortionary compensation.

In practice, lump sum compensation is difficult to design. Offering any amount as compensation to households living within some zone around a pollution source will inevitably change the number of households who want to live in that zone.

---

5. a. We have the individual marginal damage functions for the two types of residents:

   $MD_W = 2p \qquad MD_R = 6p$

   Because pollution is a nonrival bad, the aggregate marginal damage function is the vertical sum of these individual damage functions:

   $MD_T = 2p + 6p = 8p$

   b. The graph of marginal savings and aggregate marginal damage is below.

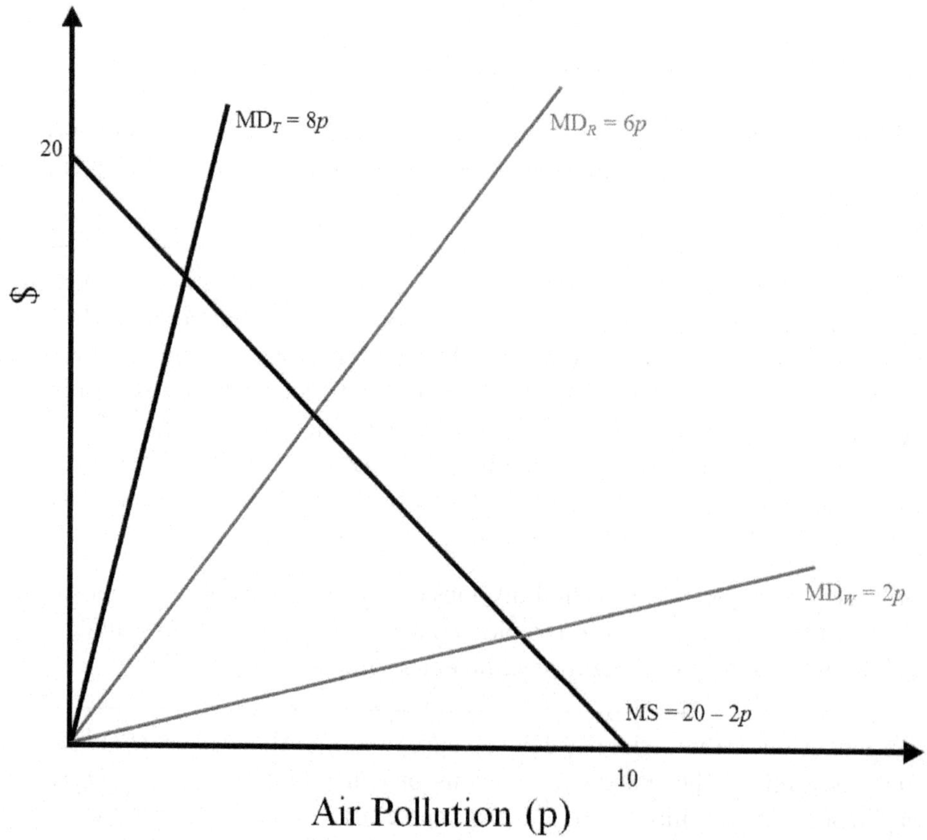

   c. In the absence of any regulation, the firm would pollute as long as the marginal savings from pollution are positive. That is, the uncontrolled level of pollution,

p^0, is found where marginal savings equals zero:

$$20 - 2p \overset{set}{=} 0 \quad \Rightarrow p^0 = 10$$

The socially optimal level of pollution, p^*, is defined by the level at which marginal savings from pollution are equal to the marginal damages from pollution:

$$20 - 2p \overset{set}{=} 8p \quad \Rightarrow p^* = 2$$

d. The uncontrolled level of pollution has been identified as $p^0 = 10$. The question asks to turn the problem around and find marginal willingness to pay (demand) for pollution *abatement*. Let abatement equal A, so that $p + A = 10$. At the uncontrolled level, marginal damages to workers are 20. Marginal willingness-to-pay for pollution *reduction* at p^0 is therefore 20. Marginal damages *fall* by 2 per unit as pollution is decreased (abatement is increased), and are zero where $p = 0$ $(A = 10)$. To transform the marginal damage (from pollution) function to a marginal willingness-to-pay (for abatement) function, substitute for pollution using $p = 10 - A$

$$\Longrightarrow \text{MWTP}_W(A) = 2(10 - A) = 20 - 2A$$

$$\Longrightarrow \text{MWTP}_R(A) = 6(10 - A) = 60 - 6A$$

$$\Longrightarrow \text{MWTP}_T(A) = 8(10 - A) = 80 - 8A$$

The marginal willingness to pay (aggregate) can also be found by the vertical summation of the Workers' and Retirees' marginal willingness to pay:

$$\text{MWTP}_T(A) = (20 - 2A) + (60 - 6A) = 80 - 8A$$

e. Since we know $p = 10 - A$ we can also substitute this identity into the Marginal Savings function to get the Marginal Cost of Abatement for the firm:

$$\text{MC}(A) = 20 - 2(10 - A) = 2A$$

The socially optimal level of abatement is 8 and is defined as the point at which the marginal cost of abatement is equal to the aggregate marginal willingness to pay:

$$\text{MC}(A) = 2A \overset{set}{=} 80 - 8A = \text{MWTP}_T(A) \quad \Longrightarrow A^* = 8$$

f. The answers to parts (c) and (e) are the equivalent. The problems of optimal provision of public bads (pollution in part (c)) and public goods (pollution abatement in part (e)) are logically the same. Problems of this type are cast in one way or the other for convenience, but the underlying objective in choosing A or p is the same: to maximize social welfare.

6. a. We can characterize the total marginal willingness-to-pay function as follows:

$$\text{MWTP}_T = \begin{cases} \text{MTWP}_R + \text{MWTP}_O = 25 - 3Q_T & Q_T \in [0, 6) \\ \text{MWTP}_O = 13 - Q_T & Q_T \in [6, 13] \end{cases}$$

The figure below is the graph of the marginal abatement cost and the total marginal willingness to pay schedules. The socially efficient level of emission reductions is 5 and is found where MTWP_T is equal to MCA.

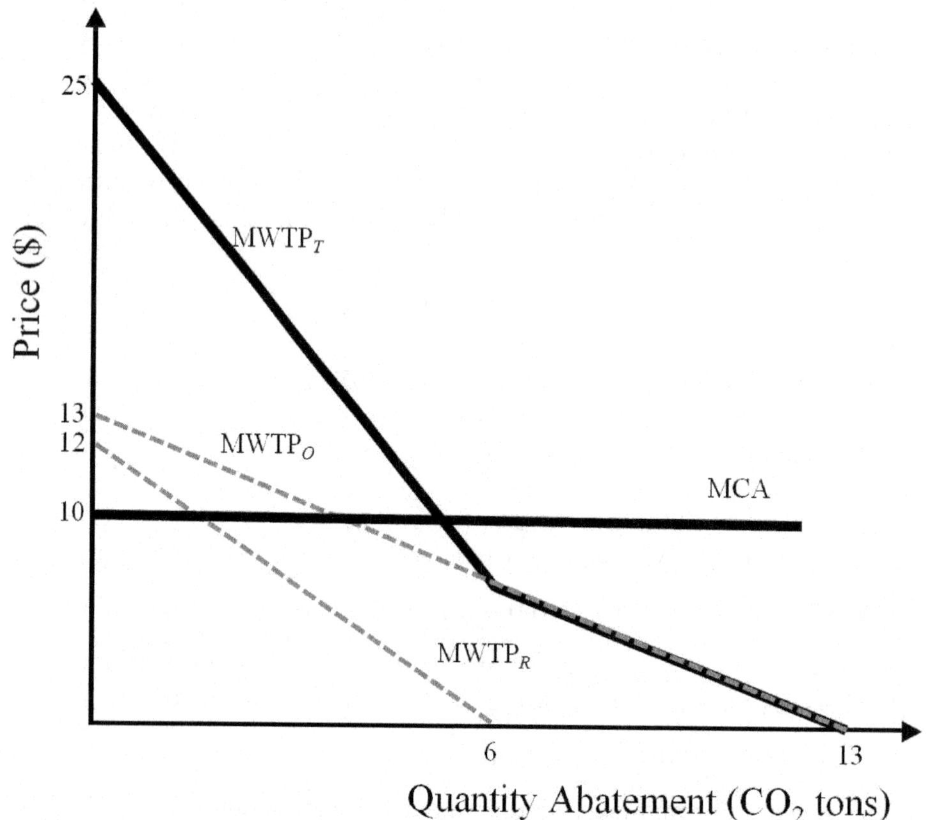

b. Under Proposal A, polluters pay each region for the damage incurred by emissions. Producers will therefore weigh the marginal cost of abatement and the marginal cost of compensation (the marginal willingness to pay of the consumers in each region). Producers will abate until them marginal cost of abatement is equal to the marginal cost of compensation:

$$\begin{aligned} \text{MCA} &\overset{set}{=} \text{MWTP}_T \\ 10 &\overset{set}{=} 25 - 3Q_T \\ &\Longrightarrow Q_T^* = 5 \end{aligned}$$

Region O and Region R would receive compensation associated with damages at $Q = 5$. This amount is the area under the MWTP curve for all units of pollution *not abated*:

$\frac{1}{2}(13-5)\cdot(13-5)=32$

And region R would receive

$\frac{1}{2}(12-2(5))\cdot(6-5)=1$

Marginal compensation is 10, the point where firms are indifferent between paying compensation and paying for abatement. The second issue is whether this outcome changes if the proposal requires payment of these damages to the UN instead of consumers in the two regions. The answer is no. From the firms' perspective, the decision regarding when to abate and when to pay compensation hinges only on total damages paid. To whom the compensation is is paid is irrelevant from the perspective of the producers.

c. Proposal B leads to a significantly different outcome, because the presumption that no reduction is undertaken in the other region is an important one. In such a case, each region negotiates with polluters as if the other region did not exist. Firms in O would abate where marginal willingness to pay is greater than 10:

$$13-Q_O \stackrel{set}{=} 10 \quad \Longrightarrow Q_O^*=3$$

Firms and consumers in O would negotiate the reduction of CO_2 emissions by 3 tons. In region R, where marginal willingness to pay is lower, we have

$$12-2Q_R \stackrel{set}{=} 10 \quad \Longrightarrow Q_R^*=1$$

Firms and consumers in R would negotiate the reduction of CO_2 emissions by 1 ton. Total reductions would therefore be 4 tons, less than the optimal amount of reduction by one ton. This result underscores the importance of collective action in the provision of public goods. Because CO_2 abatement is globally nonrival in this problem, the separate negotiation for reductions by region is analogous to private provision of a public good.

7. In Figure 5.3, individual private provision of the public good (g) is found where the line connecting the minimum points of each indifference curve (the "best response" line) intersects the line out of the origin with slope $n-1$. (Recall this is true because it is assumed everyone in this economy is identical). Consider what happens in the figure below if the number of people in the economy increases to m, where $m > n$. The line out of the origin pivots upward (becomes steeper) and the new intersection of this line and the "best-response" line is necessarily at a point associated with lower g and higher $\overline{G}$. This scenario is depicted in the figure below.

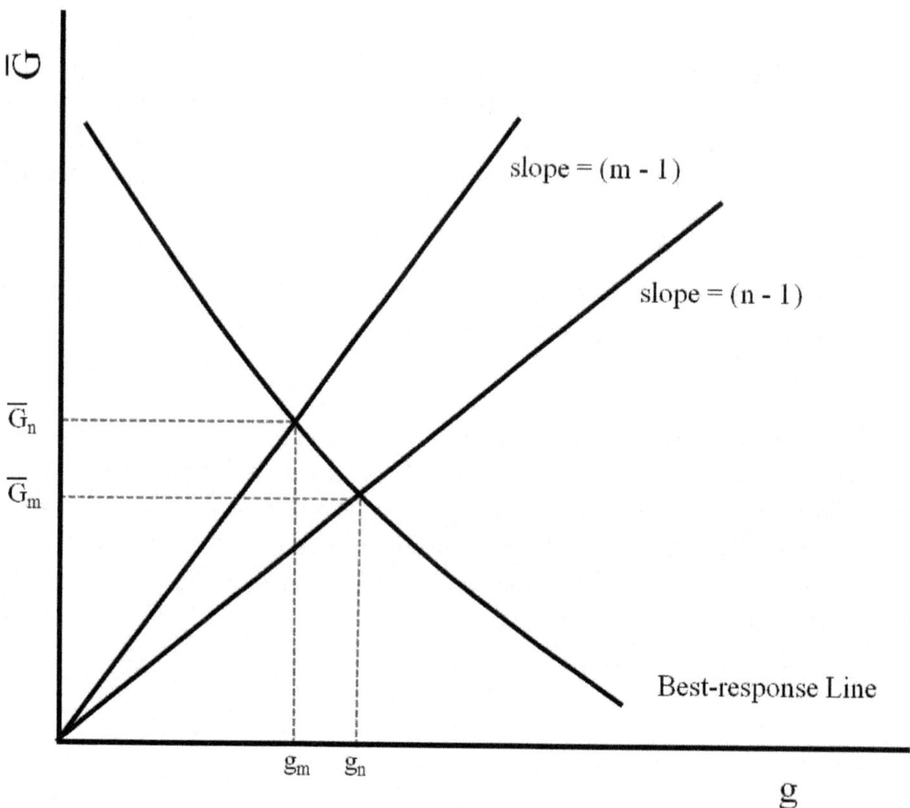

The figure below shows a set of indifference curves such that an individuals private provision of a public good increases as the number of people increases. The indifference curves have been drawn so that the minimum points are associated with higher levels of g on curves further from the origin. This reverses the slope of the "best-response" line (it now slopes upward). The intersection of the two curves still represents the optimal choice of g, and an increase from n to m still pivots the line out of the origin upward. Under these conditions, however, this increase results in an intersection associated with a greater value of g, as described in the question. The necessary condition for this outcome was an upward-sloping "best-response" line and the indifference curves that produce it.

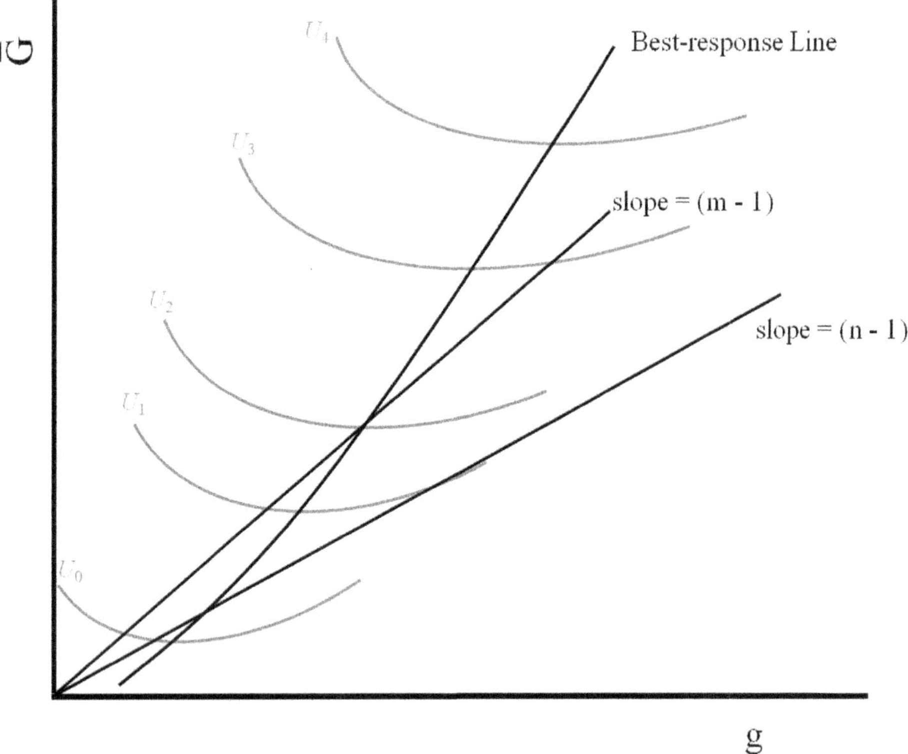

Recall how the "best-response" line was derived: for a given level of $\overline{G}$,the value of g that maximizes a single consumer's utility is at the minimum point of an indifference curve in $\overline{G} - g$ space. Begin at a point on this line, and consider what happens with indifference curves, such as those in the figure above, when $\overline{G}$ increases (for any reason). At the same level of g, the consumer now finds them self on the downward-sloping portion of a new indifference curve, suggesting that they can increase utility by purchasing more g. Such a response suggests that $\overline{G}$ and g are complements in utility. But it has already been assumed that they should be perfect substitutes in utility (they are, in fact, the same good!). This logic was incorporated in drawing the "best-response" line downward sloping in the text.

Chapter 6 Solutions

1. We will proceed by assuming that costs and benefits accrue at the end of each period.

   a. The dam is a good idea since the net present value is positive.

$$\begin{aligned}
\text{NPV}_{(a)} &= \sum \text{PV(benefits)} - \sum \text{PV(costs)} \\
&= \left[\frac{10}{0.03} \cdot \left(1 - \frac{1}{(1.03)^{50}}\right)\right] - \left[100 + \frac{5}{0.03} \cdot \left(1 - \frac{1}{(1.03)^{50}}\right) + \frac{10}{(1.03)^{50}}\right] \\
&= \$\ 26.36775 \times 10^6
\end{aligned}$$

   b. The dam is not a good idea since the net present value is negative.

$$\begin{aligned}
\text{NPV}_{(b)} &= \sum \text{PV(benefits)} - \sum \text{PV(costs)} \\
&= \left[\frac{10}{0.1} \cdot \left(1 - \frac{1}{(1.1)^{50}}\right)\right] - \left[100 + \frac{5}{0.1} \cdot \left(1 - \frac{1}{(1.1)^{50}}\right) + \frac{10}{(1.1)^{50}}\right] \\
&= \$\ -50.5111 \times 10^6
\end{aligned}$$

   c. The cutoff rate (otherwise known as the internal rate of return) is about 4.35% and can imputed by trial and error such that

$$\left[\frac{10}{r_{\text{IRR}}} \cdot \left(1 - \frac{1}{(1 + r_{\text{IRR}})^{50}}\right)\right] = \left[100 + \frac{5}{r_{\text{IRR}}} \cdot \left(1 - \frac{1}{(1 + r_{\text{IRR}})^{50}}\right) + \frac{10}{(1 + r_{IRR})^{50}}\right]$$

---

2. For this question we will proceed assuming that all costs and benefits accrue at the end of the period, and that growth (where in question) occurs from *after* the first period.

   a. Buying the woodland is not a good idea since the net present value is negative.

$$\begin{aligned}
\text{NPV}_{(a)} &= \sum \text{PV(benefits)} - \sum \text{PV(costs)} \\
&= \$\left[\frac{0.1}{0.05} \cdot \left(1 - \frac{1}{(1.05)^{50}}\right) - 2\right] \times 10^6 \\
&= \$\ -174{,}410
\end{aligned}$$

   b. In this case the maximum we would be willing to pay would be equal to the sum of the present value of benefits.

$$\begin{aligned}
\text{MaxWTP}_{(a)} &= \$\left[\frac{0.1}{0.05} \cdot \left(1 - \frac{1}{(1.05)^{50}}\right)\right] \\
&= \$1.825593 \times 10^6
\end{aligned}$$

   c. With benefits growing at 3% the purchase of the woodland now becomes a good idea since the net present value is positive. The NPV and the maximum we would be willing to pay is given below.

$$\begin{aligned}\text{NPV}_{(c)} &= \$\left[\frac{0.1}{(0.05-0.03)}\cdot\left(1-\frac{(1.03)^{50}}{(1.05)^{50}}\right)-2\right]\times 10^6\\ &= \$\ 1.088535\times 10^6\end{aligned}$$

$$\begin{aligned}\text{MaxWTP}_{(c)} &= \$\left[\frac{0.1}{(0.05-0.03)}\cdot\left(1-\frac{(1.03)^{50}}{(1.05)^{50}}\right)\right]\times 10^6\\ &= \$\ 3.088535\times 10^6\end{aligned}$$

---

3. a. The discount factor for each year is calculated as $d_t = \prod_{i=0}^{t}\left(\frac{1}{(1+r_i)}\right)$

	Year					
	0	1	2	3	4	5
Discount rate (r_i)	0	0.05	0.025	$0.016\dot{6}$	0.0125	0.01
$\frac{1}{(1+r_i)}$	1.000	0.952	0.976	0.984	0.988	0.990
Discount factor (d_t)	1.000	0.952	0.929	0.914	0.903	0.894

b. The net present value is \$6.31 and is the sum of all the discounted benefits minus the sum of all the discounted costs.

$$\begin{aligned}\text{NPV}_{hyp} &= \left[0.952\cdot\$10+0.929\cdot\$20+0.914\cdot\$30+0.903\cdot\$40+0.894\cdot\$50\right]-\$130\\ &= \$6.31\end{aligned}$$

c. Given that we hyperbolically discount the insulation is a good investment.

d. If we were a constant rate (exponential) discounter, at 5%, the the insulation would not be a good investment since the NPV would be negative for the investment.

$$\begin{aligned}\text{NPV}_{exp} &= \left[\frac{1}{(1.05)^1}\cdot\$10+\frac{1}{(1.05)^2}\cdot\$20+\frac{1}{(1.05)^3}\cdot\$30+\frac{1}{(1.05)^4}\cdot\$40\right.\\ &\quad\left.+\frac{1}{(1.05)^5}\cdot\$50\right]-\$130\\ &= \$-4.34\end{aligned}$$

---

4. a. The investment is not a good idea.

$$\begin{aligned} \text{NPV}_{a.} &= \frac{\$1 \times 10^6}{(1.1)^{100}} - \$100 \\ &= \$-27.43 \end{aligned}$$

b. The investment is a good idea.

$$\begin{aligned} \text{NPV}_{a.} &= \frac{\$1 \times 10^6}{(1.01)^{100}} - \$100 \\ &= \$369,611.21 \end{aligned}$$

c. The $\text{MaxWTP}_{2\%}$ is $\frac{\$1 \times 10^6}{(1.02)^{100}} = \$138{,}032.97$

---

5. We are given the information that the rooms in Matildastan and Tuckerville are identical, we can reasonably assume that visitors are indifferent between any choice of room either in Matildastan or Tuckerville. For simplicity we will also assume that all hotels are price takers - i.e., no given hotel can influence the price of a hotel room by restricting its own (in hotel) supply of rooms. We will also assume that visitors have perfect information about hotels and room pricing. Finally, we will assume that visitors are indifferent between one town and another whether or not streams are cleaner in one or the other (at least in regard to were they choose to get a hotel room) and that we will concern ourselves with the effects and incidence of the tax in the short run.

a. Hotel owners in Matildastan may be negatively affected by the tax if they cannot pass the incidence of the tax on to their customers or their workers. Workers and/or hotel customers in Matildastan may be negatively affected if the hotel owners can pass some or all of the tax on to them.

b. Residents of and visitors to Matildastan may be positively impacted (at least for those persons who prefer *cleaner* streams to *not-cleaner* streams). It may be that residents of and visitors to Tuckerville may also be positively impacted by the stream cleanup in Matildastan if clean streams are not pure "club goods" but have some "public goods" properties. Workers of the stream cleanup will be positively affected by the stream cleanup as long as we assume that stream worker's opportunity cost of working on stream cleanup is less the their wages and enjoyment from stream-cleaning.

c. Using the information in the text and the additional assumptions above we can graphically present the effect of a tax (t = \$10) on beds on *both* communities below.

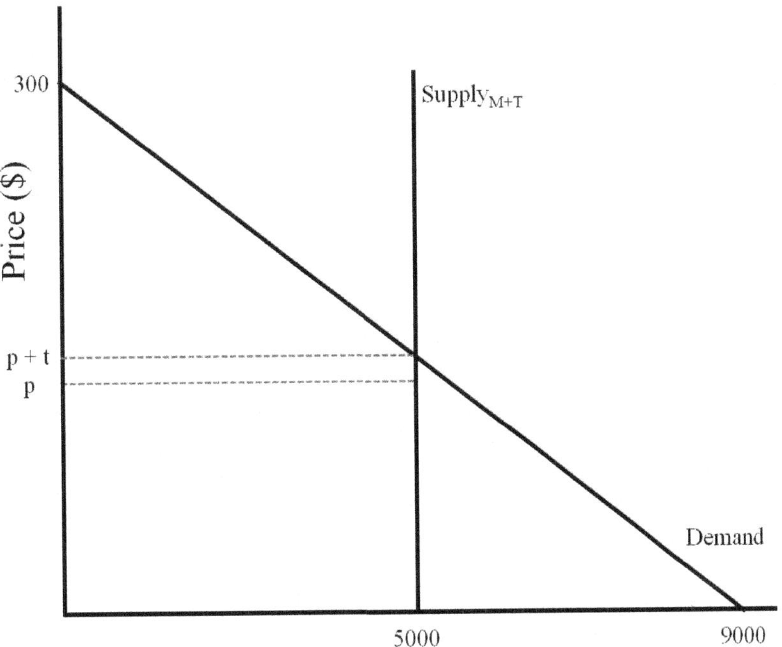

d. Since no single hotel owner in Matildastan can pass on the tax to the tourist (for the same reasons no hotel owner in Matildastan could raise their price to gain more profit before the tax), they must incur the tax burden by lowering price from p'_M to p''_M where $p''_M + t = p'_M = p'_T$.

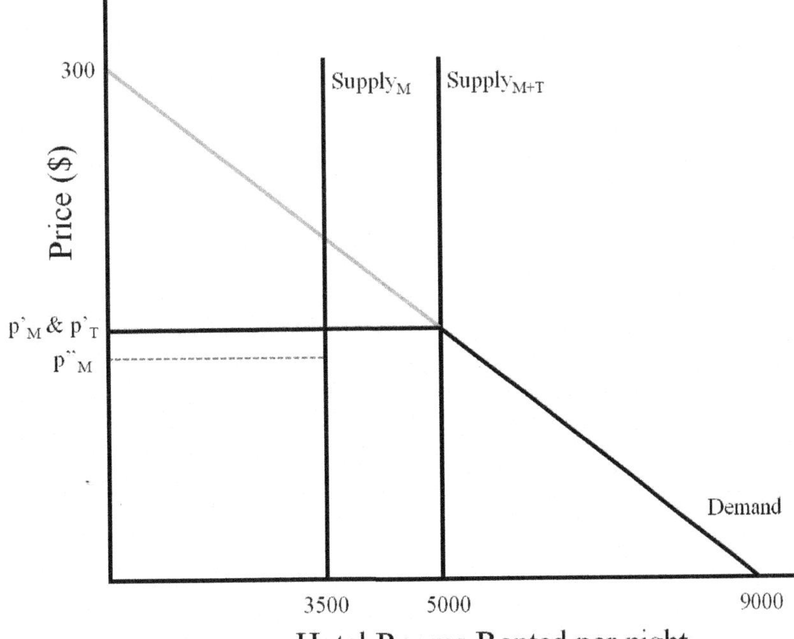

e. The incidence of the tax will fall on the hotel owners in Matildastan if we assume that labor is perfectly elastic. If the labor needed to run hotels in Matildastan is somewhat elastic then the Matildastan hotel owners and workers will share the incidence of the tax according to the degree of labor wage elasticity. If Matildastan hotel labor is perfectly inelastic, then the labor will bear the full incidence of the tax. Either way it would erroneous to think that visitors to Matildastan will pay for the stream clean-up.

---

6. By offering financing on her own terms of 0% on the nominal house price of \$3 million over the conventional 30 year term with annual payments, Millie would expect to receive annual payments of \$90,000 (due at the end of each year) - since 30 years × \$90,000 is \$2.7 million. The nominal sum of those 30 annual payments plus the 10% paid at the time of sale equals her \$3 million sale price.

   From the buyers perspective this is equivalent to Millie offering the house at a present value price of \$1.683521 million.

$$\$1.683521 \times 10^6 = \$3 \times 10^5 + \frac{\$0.9 \times 10^5}{0.05}\left(1 - \frac{1}{(1.05)^{30}}\right)$$

Chapter 7 Solutions

1. Felix's utility indifference curves are plotted below.

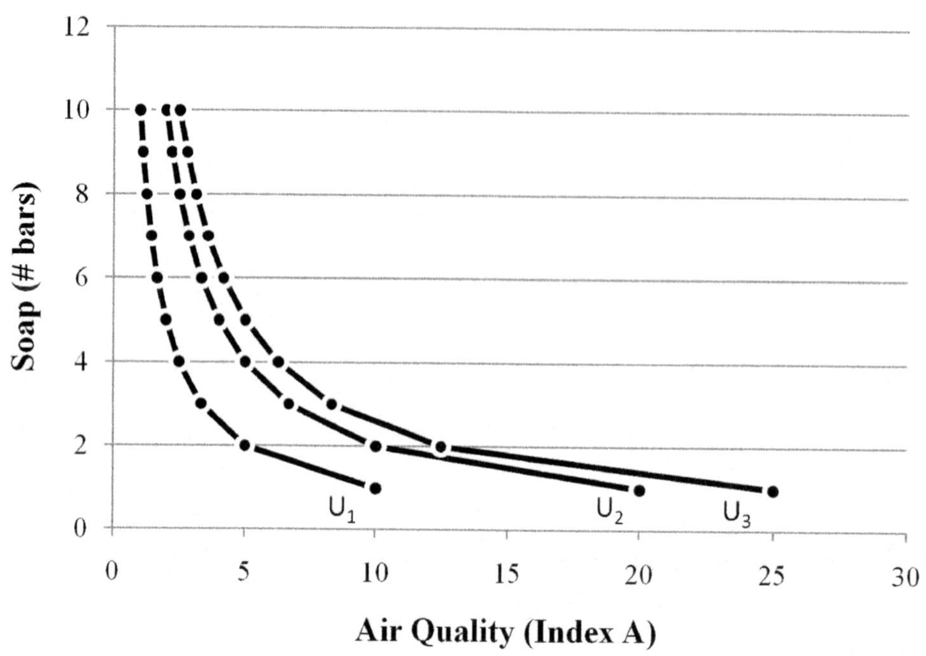

---

2. Felix begins at U_2 with the bundle (5,4) of air quality and soap, respectively. If air quality increases to 10, then to keep Felix on the same indifference curve U_2 he needs to consume the bundle (10,2) - thus he needs to consume two less bars of soap and since the price of soap is \$1 we need to take \$2 away from Felix following the *hint* from the question.

---

3. Fixing utility at 100 for the two levels of air quality effectively means we are asked to plot the two Hicksian (compensated) demand curves. Given utility is *fixed* we will solve for the compensated demand functions by first solving the consumer expenditure minimization problem then substitute that identity into the utility function and solve for P_S (the price of soap). We will then have the inverse compensated demand function to be plotted.

Min $P_S \cdot S + x \qquad st : x \cdot S \cdot A = 100$

$$\mathscr{L} = P_S \cdot S + x + \lambda(100 - x \cdot S \cdot A)$$

$$(i) \quad \frac{\partial \mathscr{L}}{\partial S} = P_S - \lambda \cdot x \cdot A \overset{set}{=} 0$$

$$(ii) \quad \frac{\partial \mathscr{L}}{\partial x} = 1 - \lambda \cdot S \cdot A \overset{set}{=} 0$$

$$\frac{(i)}{(ii)} \Rightarrow (iii) \quad P_S \cdot S = x$$

We then substitute (*iii*) into the Felix's Utility function and solve for P_S to get his inverse compensated demand function for S.

$$\begin{aligned} U &= x \cdot S \cdot A &= 100 \\ &= (P_S \cdot S) \cdot S \cdot A &= 100 \\ &\Rightarrow\ P_S = \frac{100}{S^2 \cdot A} \end{aligned}$$

For $A = 4$ and $A = 5$ and to answer the question we simply need to plot $^{25}/_{S^2}$ and $^{20}/_{S^2}$, respectively, as shown below.

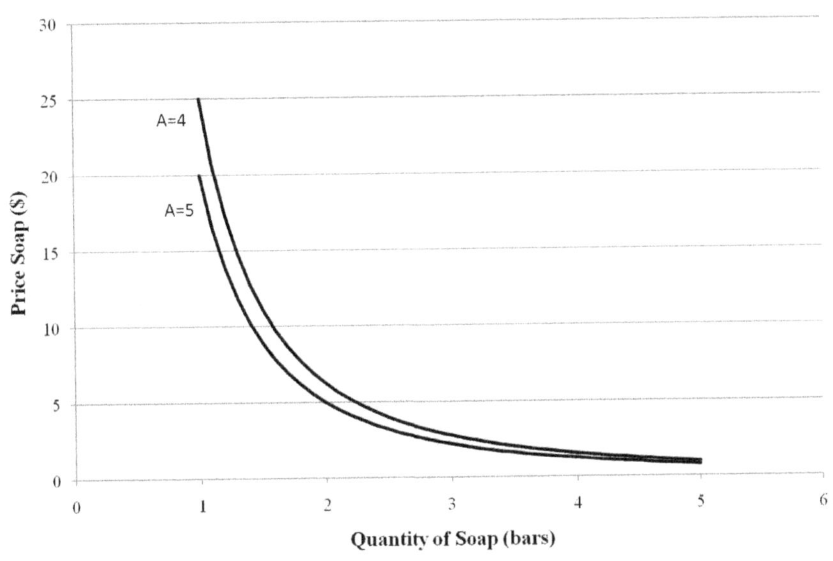

4. Answers may vary according to the creativity and imagination of the writer. A typical answer might be:

   i. Commercial fishing. This is the most direct, measurable type of use value. After the spill, the commercial fleet cannot operate for a period while the water and the stock of fish recover. Their lost profits represent direct damages from the spill.

   ii. Recreational fishing and other boating. There presumably are others who enjoy fishing or boating off the same coast, but do not do so primarily for profit. They are also damaged. This should be considered recreational use value.

   iii. Beach goers. This group suffers damage of the same type: lost recreational use value. These folks include swimmers, surfers, sunbathers, tide-pool explorers, and anyone else who would enjoy spending time along the effected coast.

   The above all represent types of use value. The more difficult element of damage to describe and measure in a case like this is from nonuse value. Each of the following two groups derive nonuse value from the condition of the French coast. The last group may also be classified as having altruistic value.

iv. Locals with concern for health of affected species and ecosystems. Even if the coast eventually recovers completely, the spill causes damage to marine species, with effects on birds and other parts of the local ecosystem. Many people have real value for the existence of this wildlife, even individual animals. They may sometimes go to observe the coastline, but this is not necessary for the value to be genuine.

v. Others (anywhere in the world) with existence value for biodiversity and ecosystem health, including those with altruistic value for the other groups listed. People living outside the effected area could have the same type of concern for the environmental health of coastal France, and could "feel the pain" of those directly damaged.

---

5. a. Jose will purchase 5 units of housing since he spends (and can only spend his money) on housing. The figure below shows Jose's indifference curve passing through the point (5,2) and his budget constraint ($\$10 \leq \$2 \cdot H$) given $A = 2$. We can easily see that the highest indifference curve Jose can afford is where $U = 10$.

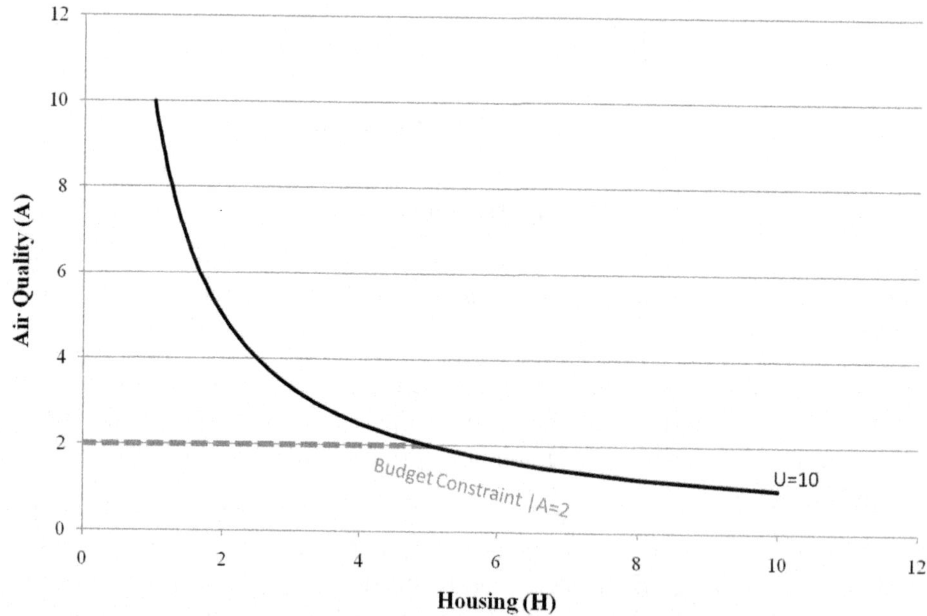

b. When $A = 4$ Jose still spends all his money on housing, buying 5 units, and attaining a utility of 20. The updated indifference curve and budget constraint is shown below.

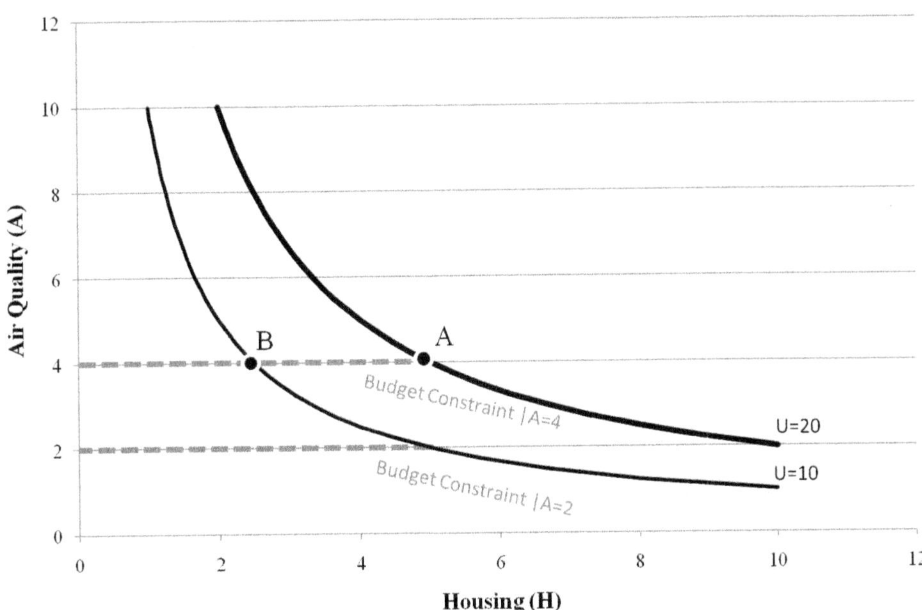

c. Jose would be willing to pay up to \$5 for air quality to increase to 4. This can be seen as \$2×the horizontal distance between the intercept of the U_{20} curve and the U_{10} curve along the second budget constraint line, a shift from point A to point B in the figure above.

Chapter 8 Solutions

1. The affected area is very small relative to the entire agricultural valley (the fraction is 5 km^2/5000 km^2, or 0.1%). This information can be used to assume that increases in output that result from cleaning up the pollution will have a negligible effect on equilibrium output, prices, and wages. Wages therefore will not change, but land rents in the effected area will increase since the cleaned up land is more productive and generates higher profits. If the assumption regarding wages and output prices above is correct, then this increase in land rents should fully reflect the benefits from pollution clean-up as long as we assume there are no other beneficial effects of the clean-up.

---

2. See the two graphs below. The first is a simple plot of the data. The second is the slope of the line between two points in the first graph plotted against the pollution midpoint. Note the marginal valuation slopes down indicating that people are willing to pay increasingly more to avoid higher levels of pollution.

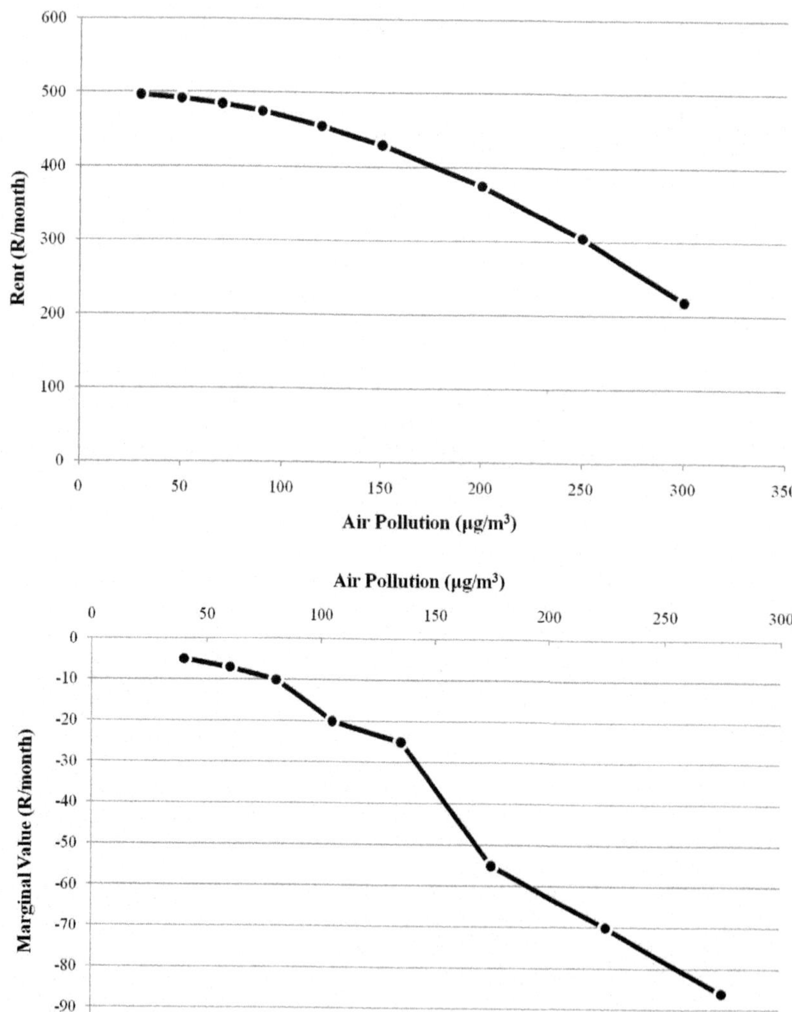

---

3. Under these circumstances, she *does* have enough information to construct a willingness to pay function for pollution; it is simply the marginal valuation of pollution found in the previous question. Notice that the (identical) people living in Novosibersk must all be indifferent between the levels of pollution and rents in different areas; otherwise they would move to the more desirable parts of town, changing the rent in both places. This is clearly not a case encountered in practice, and for this reason a typical marginal willingness-to-pay function is in general not identifiable. Figure 8.8 in the text demonstrates the issue: We only observe points on the hedonic price line $p'(z)$, but cannot find the slope of the MWTP_i functions. In Novosibersk, since everyone is identical, all points on the hedonic price line must also lie on the same MWTP curve. They are, in fact, the same function.

---

4. If we assume that people can costlessly relocate, that everyone (including Pierre) has the same preferences for pollution and other city characteristics, and that pollution has no effect on the productivity of the cities' economies, then the answer is no - Pierre is not justified in asking for a compensating increase in salary. Under the assumptions above, we would expect that housing prices are such that Pierre's reduction in consumption of other goods offsets his increase in utility that comes from living in a cleaner city. The amenity values of cities are capitalized in property values and thus in housing rental prices.

   The example from the Roback model is meant to illustrate that wages, rents, and pollution levels are all endogenously determined when people can move across cities. There is a reason that costs of living in very popular cities are higher than unpopular ones.

   Pierre could make the point that he is different from others, that he hates the beach and film festivals, etc., and therefore needs compensation for the higher prices - but then he would have to convince his potential employer that they couldn't just hire someone else who has a preference for higher environmental quality. ...

---

5. Below is a copy of Figure 7.1 from the text. The shaded area in the figure represents the total willingness to pay for a reduction in air pollution from 6 to 4 and is $\$3,750 = {}^1/_2(2 \times (\$1500 - \$2250)) + (2 \times \$1500)$.

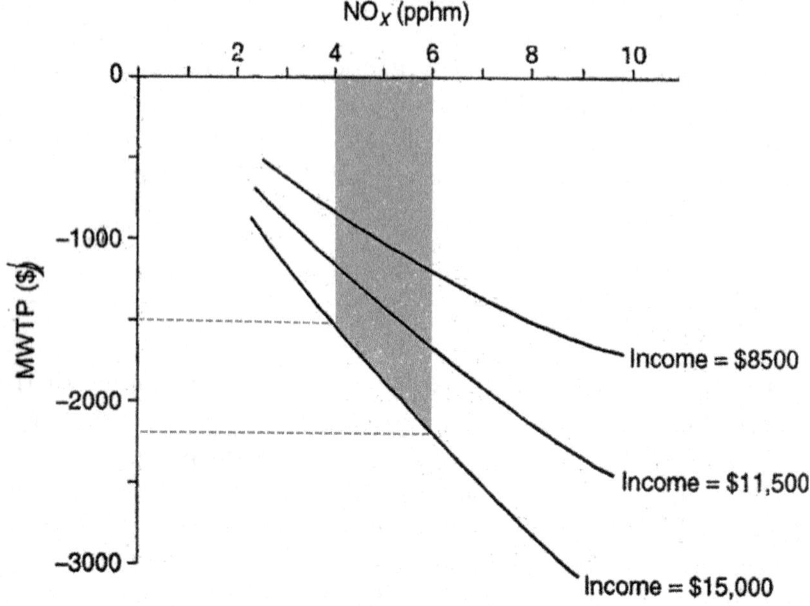

---

6. a. This is a classic application of hedonic price theory, since prices of individual car characteristics are rarely observed. We observe cars with different sets of characteristics, and we observe the prices at which they sell.

   The data in the sample collected for this study should include the sale price and as many relevant characteristics as possible for each car sold. These variables could include, but not be limited to: size, horsepower, power steering and type of brakes, model historical durability, stereo and other comfort extras, and finally fuel economy (our variable of interest).

   b. Using this data the hedonic price function for fuel economy could be estimated by multiple regression techniques - the simplest of which would be a linear regression of sale price on car characteristics. The form of the this regression model would be:

   $$car\_sale\_price_i = \hat{\beta}_0 + \hat{\beta}_1 fuel\_economy_i + \hat{\beta}_2 \mathbf{X}_i + \hat{\epsilon}_i$$

   where i indexes each observation, $\hat{\beta}_0$ is the estimator for an intercept, $\hat{\beta}_1$ is the linear effect of fuel economy on price (the hedonic price function), $\mathbf{X}_i$ is a row vector of individual car characteristics, $\hat{\beta}_2$ is a column vector of estimators for the linear effect of the characteristics in $\mathbf{X}$, and $\hat{\epsilon}_i$ is the residual from the regression.

   c. Estimating the MWTP function from the hedonic price function is considerably more difficult. See the discussion in the text.

---

7. The key to this question can be found in the text where we are told that the steepness of the firms iso-cost line represents the importance of land in the production function. If, as we are told in the question, land is not a factor in the production function, then we may reasonably conclude that the iso-cost lines as in Figure 8.2 in the text are vertical lines. Thus, if pollution is productive, then we move from point A to point B in the first figure below - indicating that in equilibrium firms must pay a higher wage to entice workers to the more polluted city, and that rental prices are also lower. If pollution is unproductive then we see from the second figure below that the equilibrium wage is lower and that land rental prices in the more polluted city are also lower as shown by the difference between point C and point D.

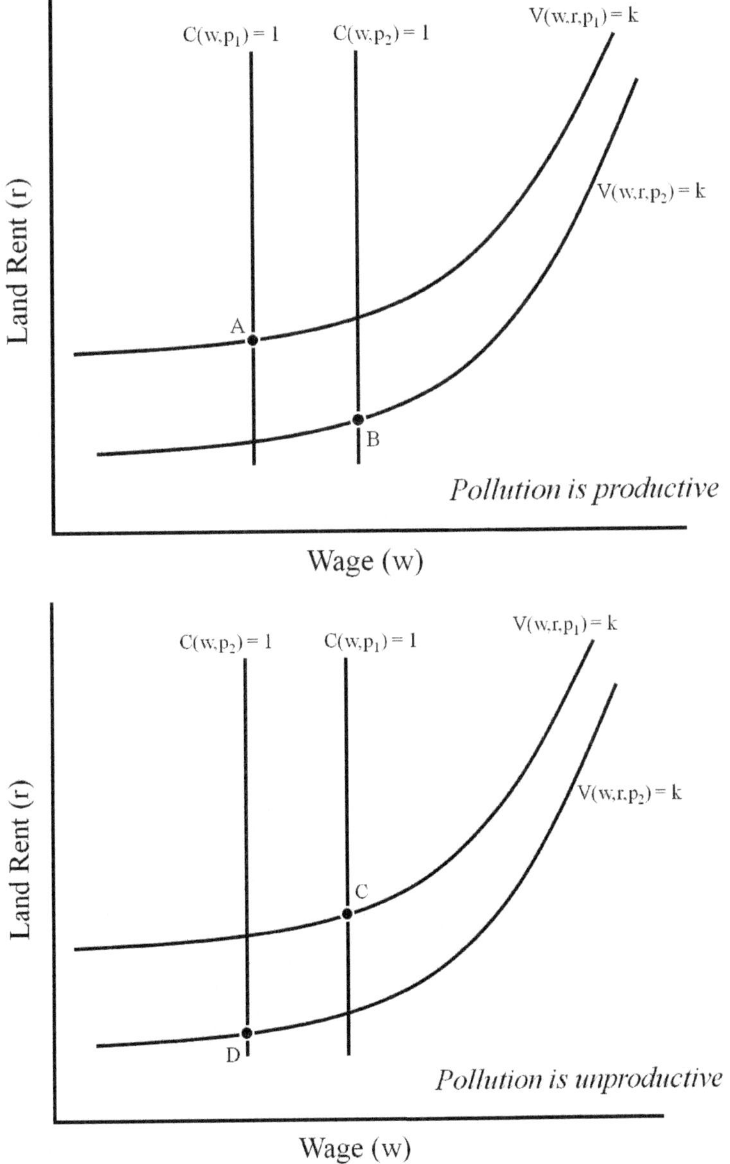

Chapter 9 Solutions

1. The objective in travel cost analyses, such as the one in this question, is to provide a convincing estimation of the demand function for beach (or park, or some other public place) visits as a function of the effective price, including travel costs. To do this, we would want to control for all of the other variables that would tend to influence demand for visits. It is generally accepted that income is such a variable, so including a variable for average income in each zone in the estimation would improve the Brittany study. Other area characteristics could be included as well, perhaps education or average age. At least some information of this nature is likely to be available from public agencies without collecting additional data directly.

---

2. We begin with the consumer utility function supposing that utility is strictly a function of hygiene (H) and the consumption of a numeraire good (x):

   $$U(H, x) = f(H, x)$$

   We shall then assume that hygiene is produced by a household production function that depends on the amount of soap used and the level of air pollution:

   $$H = g(S, P)$$

   We now state the usual budget constraint:

   $$W = p_s \cdot S + x$$

   We can now substitute to reduce the dimensionality and state the utility maximization problem as

   $$\underset{S,x}{\text{Max}}\; U\big(g(S,P), x\big) = f\big((g(S,P), x\big) \qquad s.t.\;\; W - p_s \cdot S - x = 0$$

   Continuing, we can state the Lagrangian:

   $$\mathscr{L} = f\big((g(S,P), x\big) + \lambda(W - p_s \cdot S - x)$$

---

3. a. $\underset{X,Q}{Max}\, U(X,Q) = X \cdot Q \qquad s.t.\ Y - X - P \cdot Q^2 = 0$

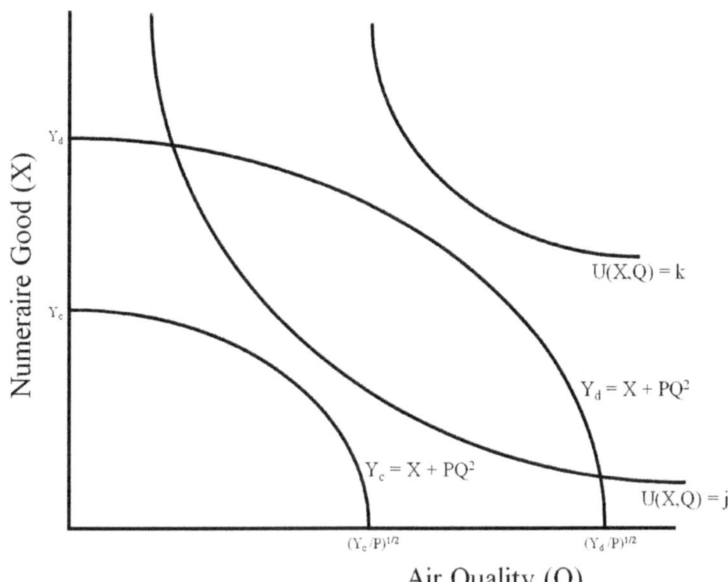

b. Where $Y = 10$ and $P = 1$, then Arturo will optimally consume the bundle $\left(6\frac{2}{3}, \sqrt{\frac{10}{3}}\right)$.

We can solve the maximization problem above by setting up the Lagrangian, or else reduce the utility function to a single variable (Q as below) and solve for the optimal amount after taking the first derivative and setting to zero:

$$\frac{\partial\,(Y - PQ^2) \cdot Q}{\partial\, Q} = YQ - 2PQ^2 \overset{set}{=} 0$$

$$\Longrightarrow Q^* = \sqrt{\tfrac{10}{3}} \qquad \Longrightarrow X^* = 6\tfrac{2}{3}$$

c. i. Where $Y = 10$ and $P = 2$, then Arturo will consume the bundle $\left(6\frac{2}{3}, \sqrt{\frac{5}{3}}\right)$

ii. Where $Y = 20$ and $P = 1$, then Arturo will consume the bundle $\left(13\frac{1}{3}, \sqrt{\frac{20}{3}}\right)$

d. We see from these results that when Arturo's income doubles, he increases (holding P constant) his choice of indoor air quality changes from $\sqrt{\frac{10}{3}}$ to $\sqrt{\frac{20}{3}}$. Thus the observation as stated that *low-income individuals are exposed to more pollution* is true in the context of this problem. It should be noted that the higher level of indoor air quality that Arturo chose $\left(\sqrt{\frac{20}{3}}\right)$ when his income was 20 was also affordable when his income was 10 - but he chose to trade off air quality for more consumption of the numeraire good. Low income Arturo in this problem is not the victim poor air quality but of his own trade-off choice.

4. a. Kakadu is a national park in Australia, we would potentially be able to observe travel to the park as a related market good. Travel cost analysis could be done observing different levels of mining activity to measure the effects of changes in "park quality."

   Park use related to visitation is not the only potential source of value. There does not appear to be an easily observable market good related to existence or other nonuse value related mining activity affecting species habitat or scenery for other Australians or even people outside the country.

   b. Attempts to measure potential effects from climate change have included observing agricultural output as a function of climate and other variables, then estimating changes in yields associated with changes in average temperature. Recreation and housing prices are also related to climate, and could be studied as well. Other effects of the climate changing may be very difficult to anticipate, much less measure.

   c. We have seen that estimating house sale price differences across different levels of pollution, controlling for other characteristics, is a way of estimating demand for air quality through a related market good. Marginal effects on health have also been used. Estimating the effect of air pollution on tourism may be another possibility.

   If a significant amount of damage from air pollution is aesthetic in nature and the damage is spread across the whole city, then this component of the damage will be more difficult to measure. Also, if pollution effects are relatively homogeneous across the city, it may not affect the prices of market goods across different parts of the city.

   d. The immediate health risks from ozone depletion could be measured through interactions with medical expenditures (more medical care associated with higher cancer rates) or defensive expenditures (more sales of sun screen and wide brimmed hats).

   The effects of long-term or permanent damage to the atmosphere on climate and ecosystems are unknown. To the extent that other damage of this type could result, it would be very difficult to observe is affect on a market good.

   e. Contamination of groundwater is also primarily a human health issue. Expenditures on medical care (from consuming contaminated water and paying for doctors) or defensive effort (consuming bottled water, treating water) could be observed. Heterogeneity in contamination of household drinking water could affect housing values across and area.

   Animals and plants could also be potentially affected by ground water contamination. Price premiums for uncontaminated produce could be measured. Concern for general ecosystem health is less easily observed with market behavior.

5. It is important to consider the availability of substitutes in the valuation of public goods and this applies particularly in regard to measuring use value. This is to say that the use value lost from the temporary closure of a beach when a perfectly identical beach only a short distance away is not closed, may be very low. Intrinsic or nonuse values aside, the *damage* caused by a beach closure may only be the extra cost in traveling to the other nearby beach (assuming beach use is not a congestable activity).

   Consumers can also substitute the consumption of the public good (in this case, going to the beach) at one point in time for consumption at a different point in time. For instance, the *damage* of a beach closure is an increasing function of the length of closure, meaning that the shorter the closure the lower the *damage*. People can simply wait until they can go to that beach again, perhaps with little inconvenience. The valuation of damages should take into account the length of time until the public good is available for use again. Failure to do so could lead us to overstate the impact of the closure.

---

6. a. If we are willing to assume that park visits are an ordinary good then we would expect that an increase in p_v to reduce v. If we are willing to assume park visits are a normal good then we would expect an increase in y to increase v.

   b. Using our results above we cannot make any predictions about how v would change with a change in w since the total effect is the result of a substitution effect and an income effect - which move in the opposite directions to each other. An increase in w raises the *opportunity cost* of park visits, with a result as above. While an increase in w raises income, with the result as above.

---

7. We begin by calculating out the total cost (per person) from each travel zone then define the demand function as the fraction of the population visiting the theme park as a function of total cost.

Zone	Distance (km)	Population	Visitors	Visitors (%)	Admission Fee	Travel Cost	Total Cost
1	10	5,000	500	10	150	10	160
2	20	10,000	900	9	150	20	170
3	30	25,000	2,000	8	150	30	180
4	40	10,000	700	7	150	40	190
5	50	100,000	6,000	6	150	50	200
6	60	500,000	25,000	5	150	60	210
7	70	200,000	8,000	4	150	70	220
8	80	50,000	1,500	3	150	80	230
9	90	100,000	2,000	2	150	90	240
10	100	100,000	1,000	1	150	100	250
		1,100,000	47,600				

From this information and the plot of the data (figure below) we can see that the demand function, expressed as a percent of the zonal population, is

$visitors\ (\%) = 26 - 0.1(total\ cost)$

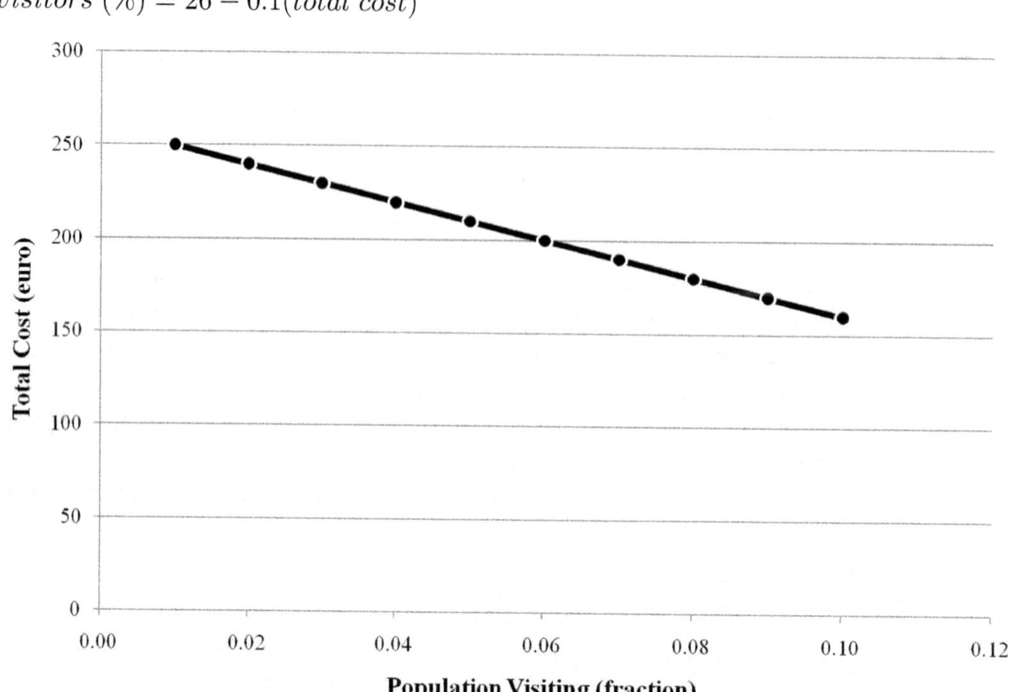

By using the demand function, changing the entry fee to 200, and reproducing the table above we can calculate the effect of a 50 euro increase in the admission fee as in the table below. From these calculations we see that a 50 euro increase in the admission fee would result in 45,000 fewer visitors.

Zone	Distance (km)	Travel Cost	Admission Fee	Total Cost	Visitors (%)	Population	Visitors
1	10	10	200	210	5	5,000	250
2	20	20	200	220	4	10,000	400
3	30	30	200	230	3	25,000	750
4	40	40	200	240	2	10,000	200
5	40	50	200	250	1	100,000	1,000
6	50	60	200	260	0	500,000	0
7	60	70	200	270	0	200,000	0
8	70	80	200	280	0	50,000	0
9	80	90	200	290	0	100,000	0
10	100	100	200	300	0	100,000	0
						1,100,000	2,600

Chapter 10 Solutions

1. Contingent valuation is generally applicable to any type of value. When asking a respondent their willingness to pay to avoid environmental damage, the motivation behind of their answer (it is hoped) is a combination of their use and nonuse value. In the case of an accident that contaminates a creek, this would include use values for those who fish, swim, collect water, or in some other way directly "use" the creek. It could also include nonuse values for those, for instance, who value the existence of the creek ecosystem in its natural state. To restrict the project a bit, a researcher might choose to concentrate on recreation value lost due to reduced fishing in the creek. This decision identifies locals who fish as the target group to be approached. The study should be designed according to the six main components of a successful CV study identified in the text:

   i. Define market scenario: The researcher could describe a plan to build a system of railings along the road to insure a truck could not crash into the creek. People would be informed that the probability of another crash (with similar effects) in the next ten years is 50:50 without the railing, and 0 with it. The county is considering installing such a system, but would need to raise local fishing license fees to fund it.

   ii. Choose elicitation method: As mentioned in the text, the NOAA Panel identifies the referendum, or discrete choice, method as the most reliable. It does require a larger sample, however, since the information from each respondent is less specific.

   iii. Design administration: In-person surveys are also recommended by the NOAA Panel, but these are the most expensive design to carry out. In addition, surveys of this type should be pretested to avoid biases associated with the interviewer. This requires additional expense.

   iv. Sample design: To collect a random sample, the researcher should draw clear borders identifying the "vicinity" of the creek, generate a list of households within the borders, and draw households randomly from the list. The identification of the sampling frame is tied to the component of demand on which the study focuses. Since the researcher has decided to concentrate on direct damages, the vicinity would perhaps be defined by communities that have direct contact with the creek.

   v. Experimental design: The payment values on the referendum are best chosen randomly, with enough variation and enough households with each value to generate statistically significant results (greater expense). It is also important to collect data on other household characteristics that will affect willingness to pay.

   vi. Estimate WTP function: The data from the survey are used to estimate WTP to eliminate the probability of another crash in the manner described in the text.

2. A resident of the United States, who lives far from Alaska, might associate a real and personal loss of value with the Exxon Valdez oil spill. This person may have specific nonuse values associated with the continuing existence of a clean and unpolluted Prince William Sound. These values may include elements of *existence, bequest*, and *altruistic* values as defined in the text. Such a person may have measurable willingness to pay (to avoid damage to Prince William Sound) and willingness to accept (to incur oil spill damage in Prince William Sound) functions. Eliciting and parameterizing these functions without bias may be problematic. The researcher may find himself or herself trying to answer a question akin to the age-old riddle: If a tree falls in a forest and no one is around to hear it, does it make a sound?

---

3. Self-selection bias will be a part of a telephone survey of households. This self-selection bias will be exacerbated if the researcher ignores the nonresponse outcomes and proceeds to base their study on the respondent group. By using a household telephone survey (assuming random selection), the researcher has selected a group within the population that lives in an identified "household" and one which has a dedicated "home" phone - probably one that is a land line. Households of this type are arguably not representative of the population. Furthermore, of that group, those who happen to be home and actually answer the phone when the surveyor calls – and who choose to take the time to carefully answer the survey are not likely to be even remotely representative of the population.

   If the source of bias is one of simple truncation or censoring then econometrics such as a Tobit model may be a statistical method to overcome the bias. Practically, a way to deal with problem may be to combine the telephone survey data with data from other response elicitation methods to try an fill in the gaps of the non-response group.

---

4. Individual answers on whether (a) your reservation buying price, and (b) your reservation selling price, are different. For most people there is generally a difference between ones willingness to pay and willingness to accept even for such banal objects as a coffee mug. These considerations should of course play a significant role in designing experiments to elicit valuations of public goods from people. Ownership and entitlement were implicit in the coffee mug scenario. The framing of the public goods valuation experiment will also implicitly imply ownership, entitlement, and often social justice - elements that will likely bias results.

Chapter 11 Solutions

1. The public interest theory of regulation views these two policy instruments as largely equivalent. Each is based on economic incentives, each attempts to have the costs of pollution reflected to the polluting firms, and each in principle is designed to satisfy the equimarginal principle and result in economic efficiency. In this normative theory of regulation efficiency is the goal. The issue of whether firms actually pay money to the government (as with a fee) or not (if issued permits) is secondary.

   The interest group theory is not so quick to dismiss the distinction between permits and fees. In this positive theory of regulation, it is noted that legislation is designed with the influence of industry lobbyists, who are not indifferent between the two types of regulation. In general, industry has been relatively more receptive to the concept of marketable permits than to emissions taxes. Permits that are freely distributed are clearly cheaper to an existing firm than a tax. This is perhaps why the former has been more commonly instituted in practice while the latter has not.

---

2. Plan A is a standard marketable permit regulation. The strength of this plan is the certainty (ignoring monitoring problems) with which total emissions can be targeted. However, while 8% total reduction is certain under Plan A, the market price at which these permits will trade is unknown. It might be the case that, if emissions reduction is very costly, the permit price could be very high - with deleterious social and political impacts that could even lead to the collapse of the permit system. Furthermore, if there are any information asymmetries, uncertainty could lead to speculative trading and price bubbles.

   In Plan B there is certainty that marginal control costs will be less than or equal to \$10 per ton of emissions abated. The trade-off is that the 8% emissions reduction is no longer guaranteed - only if the market price is less than \$10 - in which case Plans A and B are equivalent. The logic behind plan B is to provide a "safety valve" if control costs are revealed to be too high.

---

3. Tradable permits are designed to equalize marginal abatement costs across firms, thus minimizing the cost of a given pollution reduction. Where this reduction is equivalent to the reduction under technology mandates, permits are clearly preferred on this basis.

   Second, permits provide incentives for firms to reduce pollution *further*, and to find cheaper means to do so. Compliance with the technology mandate in its purest form requires only the installation of the specified equipment. This provides no incentive to find a better (cheaper) way to reduce pollution by the same amount, nor does it provide incentive for firms to invest in the research and development of equipment, processes, or practices that reduce pollution further. In fact, inventing and installing new pollution control technology would be noncompliant, since the regulation requires the use of specific equipment. A permit scheme places no restrictions of this type, allowing firms to realize savings (fewer permits needed) from finding new ways to control pollution. Research and development in the area of pollution control is therefore reasoned to be more likely under the permit system.

---

4. The "rollback" method basically requires all pollution emitters to reduce their emissions by a set percentage - say 10%. The emitters are not regulated in terms of the technology they must use and are free to reduce emissions by any means. In this way firms can internally decide their own lowest cost method to achieve the target. If all firms comply and meet their percentage reduction then the total target x_s will be achieved. One efficiency problem with this approach is that if firms are not able to trade offsetting reductions, then the inter-firm equimarginal principle is not satisfied. Furthermore, there may be informational inefficiencies in verifying every firm's compliance with the "rollback" regulation - particularly if there are a large number of small firms that must comply.

---

5. a. The agency's budget (agency surplus) is given by $B = 9Q - Q^2$ since

$$\begin{aligned} B &= \left[P_Q \cdot Q\right] - \left[w \cdot L\right] \\ &= \left[(10 - Q) \cdot Q\right] - \left[1 \cdot (Q)\right] \\ &= 9Q - Q^2 \end{aligned}$$

b. In order to plot Quantity (Q) versus Perquisites (P) we use the identity given in the text $P = B$ (since B is already net of costs we do not need $-wL$). Also, we are not told the agency head's utility function (so individual answers may vary), but in the figure below we shall assume $U(P, Q) = P^{1/2} \cdot Q$

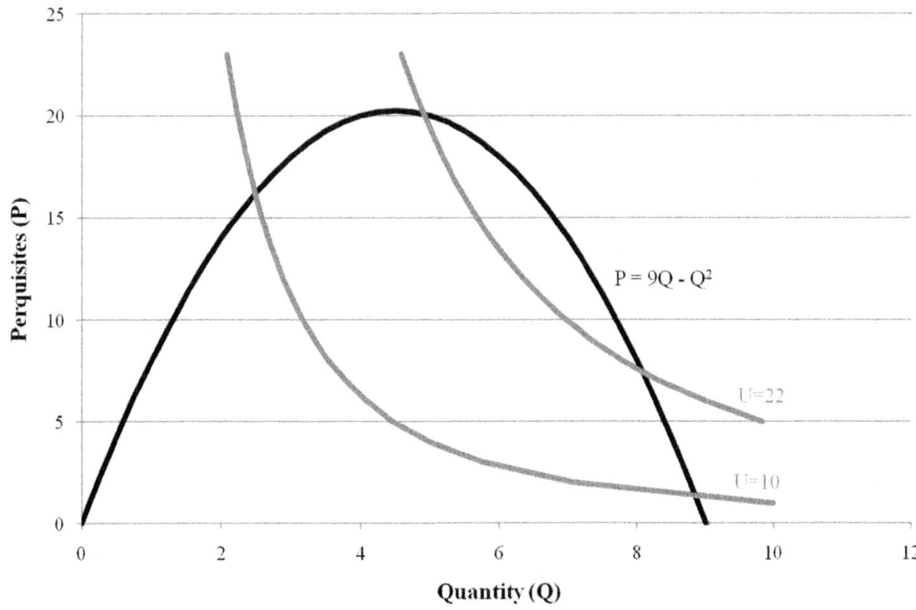

c. The profit maximizing monopolist objective function is: Max π, where $\pi = P_Q Q - wL$. After substituting, as above, we find that the profit function is equivalent to the Perquisite function. Thus a graph of the profit function would lie exactly on top the the Perquiste curve in the figure above.

d. The difference in the amount of Q produced by the Agency and the profit-maximizing monopolist comes from the fact that the monopolist only maximizes $\pi \equiv P$, while the Agency maximizes some function (the agency head's utility) across two dimensions - $P \equiv \pi$ and Q.

e. For a given Q, both the Agency and the monopolist are cost minimizers - thus their choice of L would not differ in this case.

Chapter 12 Solutions

1. a. The graph of the firm-level and aggregate marginal savings functions is below.

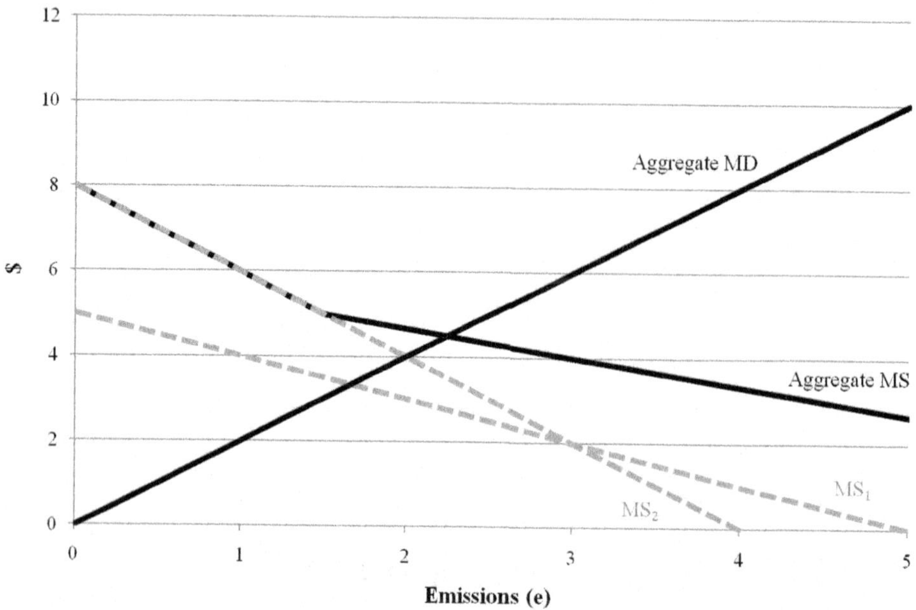

   b. The aggregate marginal damage is shown in the figure above.

   c. The optimal level of pollution is 2.25, while the appropriate Pigovian fee to produce this quantity is $4.5

   Under the Pigovian fee Firm1 will emit 0.5 units of pollution and Firm2 will emit 1.75 units of pollution.

---

2. No, not with a *true* Pigovian fee. In the text, the regulator in Section IV,B sets the fee equal to MD(s); the fee is a function of s. A *true* Pigovian fee is equal to MD *at the optimum* (at s^*). In other words, a Pigovian fee is not supposed to be a function of the level of the pollutant. Because of this difference, the monopolist in the text was in a position to manipulate the amount of the fee in changing emissions levels, leading to the second-order effect that moves the solution to the firm's problem away from the social optimum. Where the Pigovian fee is set properly, this effect is absent, and the optimum is achieved.

---

3. Efficiency does not require that the revenue collected from a Pigovian fee be distributed back to the consumers of the bad. It does not matter if the rival bad is excludable or nonexcludable. However, if the bad is rival and excludable, and perfect markets exist then the market price will be the same as a hypothetical Pigouvian fee.

---

4. a. Both firms produce rubber to the point where Price (P) = Marginal Cost (MC). Fireyear produces 15 tons of rubber, while Goodstone produces 30 tons of rubber as shown below. Fireyear makes £150 profit, and Goodstone makes £400 profit.

Fireyear	*Goodstone*
$60 = 4Q_F$	$60 = 2Q_G$
$\Rightarrow Q_F^* = 15$	$\Rightarrow Q_G^* = 30$
$\pi_F = P \cdot Q_F^* - TC(Q_F^*)$	$\pi_G = P \cdot Q_G^* - TC(Q_G^*)$
$= 60 \cdot 15 - (300 + 2(15)^2)$	$= 60 \cdot 30 - (500 + (30)^2)$
$= 150$	$= 400$

b. The Pigovian tax (t_P) should be £12 per unit. When the Pigovian tax is imposed Fireyear produces 12 tons of rubber, while Goodstone produces 24 tons of rubber as shown below. Fireyear makes a £12 loss,[1] and Goodstone makes £76 profit.

Fireyear	*Goodstone*
$60 = 4Q_F + 12$	$60 = 2Q_G + 12$
$\Rightarrow Q_F^{*t_P} = 12$	$\Rightarrow Q_G^{*t_P} = 24$
$\pi_F = P \cdot Q_F^{*t_P} - TC(Q_F^{*t_P})$	$\pi_G = P \cdot Q_G^{*t_P}$
$-T_P \cdot Q_F^{*t_P}$	$-TC(Q_G^{*t_P}) - T_P \cdot Q_F^{*t_P}$
$= 60 \cdot 12 - (300 + 2(12)^2)$	$= 60 \cdot 24 - (500 + (24)^2)$
$-12 \cdot 12$	$-12 \cdot 24$
$= -12$	$= 276$

c. We know from part (b) that if each firm internalizes the pollution damage, then their production should drop to 12 tons for Firm A and 24 tons for Firm B. Comparing this outcome with their unregulated production quantities, we see that the subsidy should result in Firm A abating 3 units, while it should result in Firm B abating 6 units. It will come of no surprise that the amount of subsidy (S_A) that results in this outcome is where S_A = £12. With the subsidy, Firm A makes £168 profit, and Goodyear makes £436 profit.

As shown below, we can calculate these numbers by defining abatement (A) as the difference between the unregulated quantity produced and the abatement subsidized quantity produced, i.e., $A = Q^* - Q^S$. By rearranging we see that $Q^S = Q^* - A$ which we can use to substitute into the cost and revenue functions given for each Firm. Then, after rearranging, we can solve for the optimal level of abatement for each firm by setting the Marginal Savings from Abatement (MS^A) equal to the Marginal Cost of Abatement (MC^A).

[1] Since Fireyear now makes a loss, some may wonder why it would not produce *zero* units - however, if it did this, we see that Fireyear's loss would increase to £300, which is certainly worse than £12.

Fireyear (Subsidized)

$$\begin{aligned}
\text{TR}_F &= 60(Q_F^* - A_F) + S_A \cdot A_F \\
&= 60(15 - A_F) + 12A_F \\
\Rightarrow \text{MR}_F &= -48 \\
\Rightarrow \boxed{\text{MC}_F^A} &= 48
\end{aligned}$$

$$\begin{aligned}
\text{TC}_F &= 300 + 2(Q_F^* - A_F)^2 \\
&= 300 + 2(15 - A_F)^2 \\
\Rightarrow \text{MC}_F &= 4(15 - A_F)(-1) \\
\Rightarrow \boxed{\text{MS}_F^A} &= 4(15 - A_F)
\end{aligned}$$

$$\begin{aligned}
\text{MS}_F^A &\overset{set}{=} \text{MC}_F^A \\
4(15 - A_F) &\overset{set}{=} 48 \\
\Rightarrow A_F^* &= 3
\end{aligned}$$

$$\begin{aligned}
\pi_F &= [\text{TR}_F] - [\text{TC}_F] \\
&= [60(12) + 12(3)] \\
&\quad -[300 + 2(12)^2] \\
&= 168
\end{aligned}$$

Goodstone (Subsidized)

$$\begin{aligned}
\text{TR}_G &= 60(Q_G^* - A_G) + S_A \cdot A_G \\
&= 60(30 - A_G) + 12A_G \\
\Rightarrow \text{MR}_G &= -48 \\
\Rightarrow \boxed{\text{MC}_G^A} &= 48
\end{aligned}$$

$$\begin{aligned}
\text{TC}_G &= 300 + (Q_G^* - A_F)^2 \\
&= 300 + (30 - A_F)^2 \\
\Rightarrow \text{MC}_G &= 2(30 - A_G)(-1) \\
\Rightarrow \boxed{\text{MS}_G^A} &= 2(30 - A_G)
\end{aligned}$$

$$\begin{aligned}
\text{MS}_G^A &\overset{set}{=} \text{MC}_G^A \\
2(30 - A_G) &\overset{set}{=} 48 \\
\Rightarrow A_G^* &= 6
\end{aligned}$$

$$\begin{aligned}
\pi_G &= [\text{TR}_G] - [\text{TC}_G] \\
&= [60(24) + 12(6)] \\
&\quad -[300 + (24)^2] \\
&= 636
\end{aligned}$$

d. The unregulated outcome in (a) is inefficient because of the pollution externality. The objective of the Pigovian fee applied in (b) was the socially optimal combination of output and emissions. The production outcome in (c) is the same as in (b) but in the long run, Fireyear would leave the industry where an emissions fee is levied, but would remain in business under a subsidy program (since $\pi_F(tax) < 0$, $\pi_F(subsidy) > 0$).

The Pigovian fee results in the socially efficient level of emissions because it causes firms to internalize the social costs associated with producing rubber. This process is also present with a subsidy program, but provides transfers to each firm. This transfer is distortionary in that it supports the continued operation of firms that could not operate profitably if the social costs were internalized. We can therefore deduce that the solution in (b) is optimal, while the solution in (c) is not.

5. a. To maximize profit, the factory sets Marginal Revenue (Price) equal to Marginal Cost (including the tax) and produces 3 tons of mashed potatoes.

$$\begin{aligned} 10 &\overset{set}{=} 2Q+4 \\ \Rightarrow Q^* &= 3 \end{aligned}$$

The factory then emits $3 \cdot 2 = 6$ units of pollution and pays $\$2 \cdot 6 = \$12$ in fees. The factory's profit is $\$10 \cdot 3 - \$3^2 - \$12 = \$9$.

b. The firm would be willing to pay up to \$7 for the pollution reducing device. Since the factory's optimal output would increase to 4 tons, its profit would increase to \$16 if it were given the device for free. The difference between the profit in (a) and \$16 is the most the factory would be willing to pay.

c. If there was no government intervention the factory would not be willing to pay anything for the pollution reducing device. Clearly, if factory is unregulated, their profit does not depend on the pollution reducing device, because they are not paying for pollution emitted. This reveals a small part of the dynamic nature of regulation: a fee initially reduces pollution, but then generates demand for pollution reducing equipment, which can further reduce pollution. Such devices would not be invented, developed, or produced when demand does not exist.

---

6. The outcome in Figure 12.7 in the text is an example and *does not* always have to be the case. In the figure below, the same scenario is depicted, but here the effect of monopoly power on the reduction of output is less than the effect of the externality on the efficient level of output. The price–quantity combination (P_U, S_U) is associated with the unregulated monopolist (at this point, marginal revenue equals marginal private cost). S^* represents the socially optimal output level, at which price equals marginal social cost. In the diagram, $S_U > S^*$.

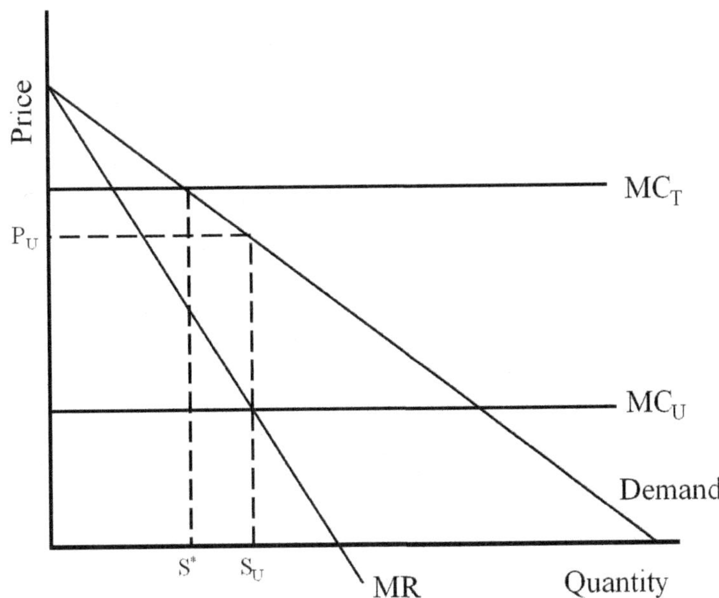

Which level of output, S_U or S^*, is greater depends on the relative magnitude of each market failure. S_U is determined by the elasticity of demand, and S^* is determined by this same elasticity and the size of marginal external cost. Theoretically, these market failures could offset each other perfectly, and the unregulated monopolist would produce the efficient amount. This is exceptionally unlikely, however, since there is no logical connection between the magnitude of monopoly power and the magnitude of the externality.

---

7. From the text, the tax interaction and revenue recycling effects can be expressed as

$$IE = \frac{(1+V) \cdot t_L \cdot t_X \cdot \eta_{HX} \cdot H^*}{P_X}$$

$$RE = V \cdot t_X \cdot X^+$$

The expression we want to achieve for the ratio of these two involves η_{XH}, and not η_{HX}, so it will be necessary to substitute the former for the latter:

$$\eta_{HX} = \tfrac{\Delta H}{H} \cdot \tfrac{P_X}{\Delta P_X} \Longrightarrow \tfrac{\Delta H}{\Delta P_X} = \frac{H \cdot \eta_{HX}}{P_X}$$

$$\eta_{XH} = \tfrac{\Delta X}{X} \cdot \tfrac{w}{\Delta w} \Longrightarrow \tfrac{\Delta X}{\Delta w} = \frac{X \cdot \eta_{XH}}{w}$$

These last two expressions have to be equal to each other by the symmetry of the Slutsky matrix. So

$$\frac{H \cdot \eta_{HX}}{P_X} = \frac{X \cdot \eta_{XH}}{w} \Longrightarrow \eta_{HX} = \frac{P_X \cdot X \cdot \eta_{XH}}{w \cdot H}$$

Substituting this into the expression for IE above and simplifying yields

$$IE = \frac{(1+V) \cdot t_L \cdot t_X \cdot \eta_{XH} \cdot X^*}{w}$$

Taking the ratio of this expression and the expression for RE, we obtain

$$\tfrac{IE}{RE} = \frac{(1+V)}{V} \cdot \frac{t_L \cdot \eta_{XH} \cdot X^*}{w \cdot X^+}$$

Use the expression given in the problem: $V = \dfrac{t_L \cdot \varepsilon}{[w - t_L \cdot \varepsilon]}$

$$\tfrac{IE}{RE} = \frac{[w - t_L \cdot \varepsilon + t_L \cdot \varepsilon]}{t_L \cdot \varepsilon} \cdot \frac{t_L \cdot \eta_{XH} \cdot X^*}{w \cdot X^+}$$

$$= \frac{\eta_{XH} \cdot X^*}{\varepsilon \cdot X^+}$$

So when $\eta_{XH} = \varepsilon$, the ratio of the tax interaction and revenue recycling effects is simply the ratio of the pre- and post-tax levels of X. This is very useful information for policy makers, who are interested in the relative magnitudes of these effects and can observe X^{+} and X^{*} directly. For instance, since $X^{*} > X^{+}$ (for a tax increase), when $\eta_{XH} = \varepsilon$ it must therefore be the case that $IE > RE$.

Chapter 13 Solutions

1. Where no property right to clean air exists, none of the coalitions $A1 - A5$ are stable. To demonstrate this, it can be shown that for each coalition, for any division of the profits, there exists *another* coalition that is more attractive to two members. It is trivial for A1: any of the four coalitions would be preferred by at least two members. For each of the others:

   $A2: \quad \{(R, S), (L)\} \quad \{\$15, \$24\}$

   The mill will require at least \$8 to prefer this to independent action. Suppose the distribution of profits is $(R: \$7, S: \$8)$. This is not a stable coalition, since A4 provides a coalition where the mill and the laundry are better off by merging: together they make \$36, which could be allocated $(S: \$11, L: \$25)$. This suggests these two would "defect" from A2.

   $A3: \quad \{(R, S, L)\} \quad \{\$40\}$

   This is the "grand coalition." A division of the profits that each firm would prefer to independent action would be $(R: \$4, S: \$9, L: \$27)$. This also is not a stable coalition, since $A2$ would provide an opportunity for the railroad and the mill to improve their payoffs by "defecting." By merging, that coalition allows them to make \$15, which could be divided $(R: \$5, S: \$10)$.

   $A4: \quad \{(R), (S, L)\} \quad \{\$3, \$36\}$

   The \$36 payoff for the merged mill-laundry could be divided $(S: \$11, L: \$25)$; each prefers this coalition to independent action. $A5$ will provide the coalition-buster this time: by defecting from $A4$ and merging together, the railroad and the laundry can improve their payoffs. Together they would earn \$31 under such an arrangement, which could be divided $(R: \$4, L: \$27)$.

   $A5: \quad \{(R, L), (S)\} \quad \{\$31, \$8\}$

   Suppose the division of profits described above prevails: $(R: \$4, L: \$27)$. The reverse defection could take place, since A4 provides a coalition between the laundry and mill that produces joint profits of \$36. The division $(S: \$9, L: 27)$ would be (weakly) preferred by these two firms.

   The point of this exercise is to demonstrate the concept of the empty core. The above are only examples, but it can be verified that there exists no distribution of the coalition profits that provides a stable coalition.

2. a. The efficient outcome is where the fishery is located downstream of the mill and the treatment plant is built. This results in a total joint profit of $800.

   b. The four outcomes are tabulated below.

	Right to pollute		Right to clean	
	Mill	Fishery	Mill	Fishery
Fishery upstream	$500	$200	$300	$300
Fishery downstream	$500	$100	$300	$500

   c. The no-bargain solution in the case where the Mill has the right to pollute is the upper-right cell in the payoff matrix ($500 $200). With costless bargaining, the Fishery could offer to purchase the equipment for the Mill. The efficient outcome will then result since the increase in profit to the Fishery where the pollution control is installed (and they move downstream) is $300, which is greater than the $200 needed to cover the costs of the equipment for the Mill.

---

3. The text argues that the relevant concepts of market failure related to pollution (it is a *public bad* or it produces an *externality*) are logically redundant. Furthermore, it has established that in the absence of market failure, pollution would be allocated efficiently as goods and bads are in well-functioning markets. In the words of chapter 5, pollution levels would be "Pareto irrelevant" if these market failures did not exist. The validity of the statement therefore hinges on the extent to which the market failures associated with pollution arise from issues of property rights.

   Why are there no markets that arise to optimally price and allocate pollution? Economists would tend to agree that the *proximate* cause for the market failure is the absence of clearly defined and/or enforceable property rights. In this sense, the statement in the question is quite true. The very important omission of this statement is regarding the *ultimate* cause of market failure. There are very fundamental reasons why property rights are defined and enforced for some goods and bads and not others. In the case of non-point source pollution, the characteristics of non-rivalry and nonexcludability are fundamental to the bad and these characteristics limit the capacity of government to define and enforce property rights and resolve disputes. It is for this reason that a stronger statement that pollution problems are *merely* a failure of government to define and enforce property rights is a bit simplistic.

---

4. a. The number of shoes and baked goodies the merged firm makes when $P_S = 8$ is 2 and 4, respectively, while the number of shoes and baked goodies the merged firm makes when $P_S = 14$ is 6 and 2, respectively.

   We can solve the maximization problem for the combined firm by first merging the two cost functions to make a combined Cost Function. Then take the derivative of the combined cost function with respect to baked goods and shoes to get marginal cost functions for those two goods. We then set each of these two cost functions equal to their respective prices (marginal revenue) and solve as a system of simultaneous equations.

$$\begin{aligned} C_{SB}(S,B) &= [C_S(S)] + [C_B(B,S)] \\ &= [S^2+8] + [B^2 + BS + 8] \\ &= S^2 + B^2 + BS + 12 \\ \Rightarrow \text{MC}_B(S,B) &= 2B + S \\ \Rightarrow \text{MC}_S(S,B) &= 2S + B \end{aligned}$$

$$\begin{aligned} 2B + S &\stackrel{set}{=} P_B & &\Rightarrow (i) \quad S = P_B - 2B \\ 2S + B &\stackrel{set}{=} P_S & &\Rightarrow (ii) \quad S = \tfrac{1}{2}(P_S - B) \\ (i) &= (ii) & &\Rightarrow (iii) \quad \boxed{B^* = \frac{2}{3}\left(P_B - \frac{1}{2}P_S\right)} \qquad (P_B \geq \tfrac{1}{2}P_S) \end{aligned}$$

$P_S = 8$			$P_S = 14$		
B^*	$=$	$\frac{2}{3}(10 - \frac{1}{2}(8))$	B^*	$=$	$\frac{2}{3}(10 - \frac{1}{2}(14))$
	$=$	4		$=$	2
$\Rightarrow S^*$	$=$	2	$\Rightarrow S^*$	$=$	6

b. If Finch's Footwear has the right to pollute, then they will maximize profit without regard their impact on the bakery as shown below. Millie's Muffins will also profit maximize but take the level of pollution from the shoe factory as given. The number of baked goods and shoes produced when $P_S = 8$ is 3 and 4, respectively. The number of baked goods and shoes produced when $P_S = 14$ is 1.5 and 7, respectively.

$P_S = 8$			$P_S = 14$		
Finch's Footwear			*Finch's Footwear*		
$2S$	$\stackrel{set}{=}$	8	$2S$	$\stackrel{set}{=}$	14
$\Rightarrow S^*$	$=$	4	$\Rightarrow S^*$	$=$	7
Millie's Muffins			*Millie's Muffins*		
$2B + 4$	$\stackrel{set}{=}$	10	$2B + 7$	$\stackrel{set}{=}$	10
$\Rightarrow B^*$	$=$	3	$\Rightarrow B^*$	$=$	1.5

c. Given that Millie's Muffins has the right to clean air, the bakery will produce output to maximize profit as if $S = 0$ and make 5 units of baked goods for \$21 profit. If the shoe company wishes to produce output, it must compensate Millie's Muffins such that Millie's Muffins makes at least \$21 profit.

For every unit of output the shoe company produces Millie's Muffins profit drops by \$5. We see this by the fact that $\partial\pi_B/\partial S = -B$ and we know Millie's will make 5 units of B. Thus Finch's Shoes marginal cost becomes $MC_S = 2S + 5$. Finch's produces output such that price equals marginal cost and makes 1.5 units of shoes if $P_S = 8$ and 4.5 units of shoes if $P_S = 14$.

Accordingly, Finch's pays \$7.50 in compensation to Millie's if $P_S = 8$, and it pays \$22.50 compensation if $P_S = 14$.

d. By comparing the total profit in each of the three scenarios above we find that, for either $P_S = 8$ or $P_S = 14$, total profit is highest when both firms are combined. This means that the optimal outcome is attained under neither the assignment of property rights to Finch's nor the assignment of property rights to Millie's. Therefore we must conclude that the initial allocation of the right to pollute or the right to clean air does matter, contrary to the Coase Theorem in this example.

---

5. This is a standard comparison between a command-and-control based regulation (Plan A) and an economic incentive based regulation (Plan B). In general, economists prefer the latter category on the grounds of economic efficiency as outlined below.

   i. The equimarginal principle is more likely to be achieved with Plan B. This plan is designed so that trucks observe a marginal cost from generating pollution: each unit of pollution results in foregone tax benefits. Where the cost of reducing emissions is less than the tax benefit, the trucking company is expected to undertake the abatement activity. If all companies face the same tax incentives, total abatement activity will differ across firms (based on age and condition of trucks, etc.), but the marginal cost of pollution control should be the same. This is a necessary condition for cost-effective pollution reduction.

   ii. Plan B provides an incentive for firms to find ways to lower emissions. Plan A requires specific equipment and procedures, so compliance involves simply following the rules. Plan B allows firms to save money if they can innovate and discover new pollution control methods. The magnitude of this second effect is debatable, but in some cases it is believed to be very important.

   There are other issues though: political viability, enforcement, and fairness, to name three. One strength of command-and-control regulation is that it is relatively easy to enforce. The regulator does not have to actually observe emissions, as would be required for Plan B. The issues of viability and fairness are entangled. Lobbying from business groups creates strong opposition to regulation that is costly to firms, but many voters generally react negatively to what may seem like *pandering to polluters*.

---

6. (a) If the beekeeper acts independently then 5 hives will be maintained. As a profit maximizer the beekeeper will maintain hives up to the point that marginal cost equals marginal revenue:

$$\begin{aligned} \text{MC}_H &\overset{set}{=} P_H \\ 10 + 2H &= 20 \\ \Rightarrow H^* &= 5 \end{aligned}$$

(b) The socially efficient number of hives is 10. Since each hive also conveys the benefit of pollinating the orchard that would otherwise have cost \$10, the marginal public benefit is therefore \$10, which we can add to the marginal private benefit (marginal revenue) to get a marginal social benefit function.

$$\begin{aligned} \text{MC}_H &\overset{set}{=} MB_H(\text{social}) \\ 10 + 2H &= 30 \\ \Rightarrow H^{S*} &= 10 \end{aligned}$$

(c) The benefit to the orchard owner is $(10 - 5) \cdot \$10 = \$50$. The cost (in lower profit) to the beekeeper of increasing the number of hives from 5 to 10 is

$\pi_B(H = 10) = 20(10) - 10(10) - (10)^2 - 10 = \$ - 10$

$\pi_B(H = 5) - \Pi_B(H = 10) = \$25$

The benefits to the orchard owner outweigh the costs to the beekeeper by \$25. This suggests that the orchard owner could offer the beekeeper anywhere between \$25 and \$50 to increase output from 5 to 10 hives, and both would be better off.

How do we know they would settle at this (efficient) solution? The answer is the key to the Coase Theorem. For the sixth through tenth hives produced, the marginal benefit to the orchard owner (constant at \$10) was larger than the reduction in profits to the beekeeper. We can also verify that the eleventh hive would cost more to the beekeeper in foregone profit than \$10. This, in fact, is what defines $H = 10$ as the efficient outcome.

(d) If total transaction costs were $\geq$ \$25, then all gains from arrangement in (c) would be erased. We can easily see this in the following case. If the beekeeper accepted just lost profit from increasing hives from 5 to 10, then the orchard owner would necessarily pay \$25 to the beekeeper. The surplus to the orchard grower from this arrangement would be \$50 - \$25 = \$25. Thus if total transaction costs were $\geq$ \$25, then all the surplus from trade would be lost.

7. a. The centralized decision making within a company should make transactions costs lowest for internal trades. Considerations of compensation, presumably the primary topic of negotiations, are absent when the same firm observes all the costs and benefits of a trade.

   The *existence* of brokered transactions is strong evidence that those transactions have lower overall transaction costs than unbrokered external trades. If simply finding someone with whom to trade is a problem, an intermediary who specialized in arranging trades could be very efficient. So, from lowest transaction costs to highest, we would expect the order to be: internal, brokered, external.

   b. There is some evidence in the data that support the hypothesis in a. Since the question claims that low trading volume indicates higher transaction costs we cannot tautologically conclude that there must me higher transaction costs since there are low numbers of trades. But there may be some information in the relative composition of the trading data. Consider the pollutants with the fewest number of total trades: CO, PM, and SO_X. These pollutants saw 12 internal trades, 13 brokered trades, and only 2 external trades. Compare this to the more heavily traded pollutants: NO_X and VOC. These saw 36 internal trades, 76 brokered trades, and 65 external trades. Internal trades may be cheap, but their number is limited by the size of firms and the allocation of pollution within firms. This accounts for internal trades making up only 20% of transactions in the "heavily traded" pollutants. Internal trades, in contrast, make up 44% of transactions in "thinly traded" pollutants. Higher transactions costs for thinly traded pollutants suggests that external and brokered trades are frequently too difficult to arrange, even when they would be mutually desirable.

   With respect to trades between firms, the ordering in part (a) suggested that brokered trades are cheaper than external trades. This should be especially true if the hypothesis is correct that transaction costs are higher because of the difficulty of finding trading partners. In the "heavy" group, external trades accounted for 37% of transactions. In the "thin" group, this fraction is only 7%.

   So the data suggest that more expensive trades are less likely to take place in thinly traded pollutants. This is consistent with the hypothesis that between firm transactions costs will be higher in this group.

   c. In the pollution trading market place where, if search costs make up the bulk of the transaction costs, then firms hoping to sell a certain volume of pollutants need to find a matching firm willing to buy that certain volume - a double coincidence of wants. If we were to graph the frequency of the double coincidence of wants by size of the trade, we might see that finding another firm that wants to just trade a very small volume might be difficult (assuming search costs are independent of the size of the trade). Similarly, finding another firm that wants to trade a very large volume might also be difficult. There may be a median trade size that many firms want to make and it might be relatively easy to make these trades. We might expect that for small volumes, firms may opt to simply internally trade and thus avoid brokering fees on such a small trade or the relatively high search cost of finding another firm that wants just a small trade. We also might expect that a firm wanting to trade a large volume might look to a broker to make a trading match, being unable or unwilling to internally trade a large volume and unwilling to commit to the search costs of finding another firm looking to make a large trade. This is just one scenario, but generally we might think that it is more likely that small volume trades will occur internally.

---

8. The "offset system" is tantamount to a marketable permit system. First, existing firms are given the de facto property right to emit pollution just as firms are given permits, or the right to emit pollution, in the marketable permit system. Second, new firms must convince, or in other words compensate, existing firms to reduce pollution so that they may have the right to emit pollution on a one-for-one basis - just the same as a firm in the marketable permit system must pay another firm on a one-for-one basis for permits if it wants to emit more pollution. So in both cases, property rights are assigned, quantity is capped, and trading is allowed to take place.

---

9. a. The efficient, or first-best, solution is achieved when pollution tax is set at $15. This results in the optimal level of 15 tons of pollution abatement as shown in the figure below.

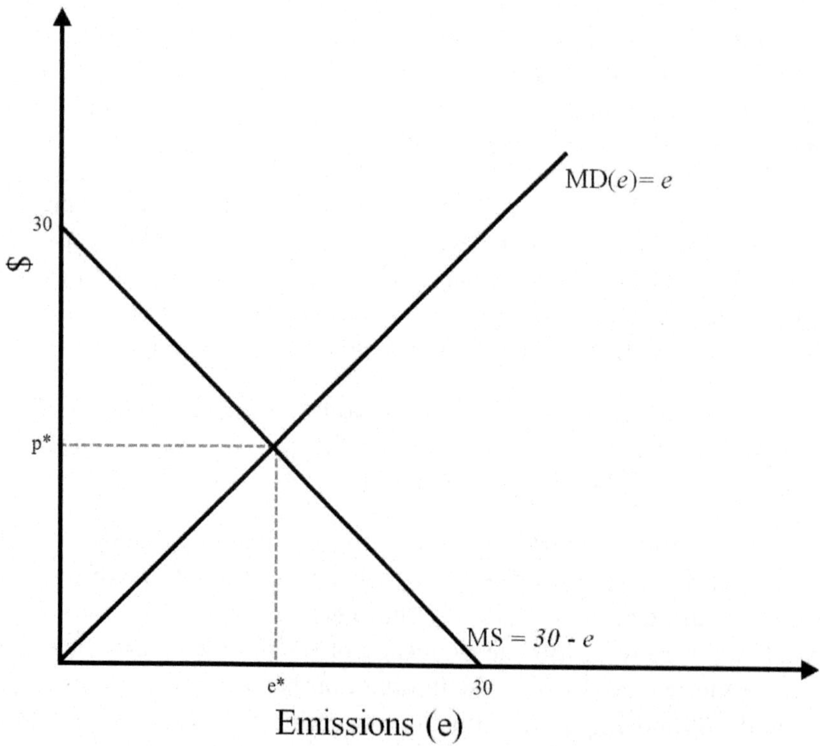

b. Given the information that indicates we are in a second-best world, we know that every ton of emissions reduced results in $10 of welfare loss (due to the fact that pre-existing taxes are distortionary) the marginal damage of emissions should therefore be reduced by \$10 to reflect the fact that we avoid the welfare loss by not abating. Alternatively, we could adapt the industry marginal savings function to become a social marginal savings function by adding \$10 to the $MS(e)$ function given. Either way, and as seen graphically below, the second-best solution now becomes 10 tons of abatement resulting in 20 tons of marketable permits to be allocated free of charge.

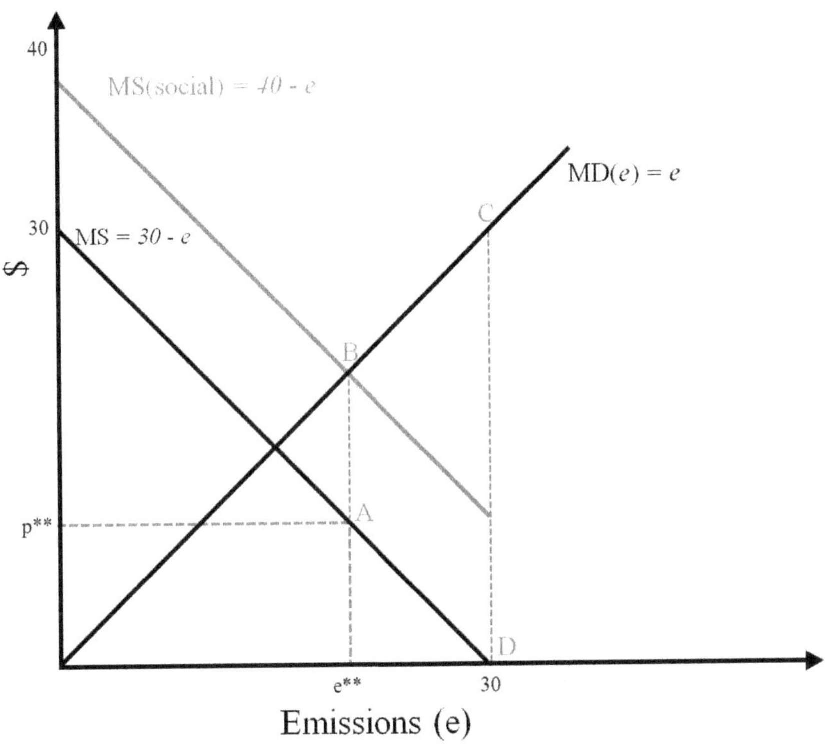

c. We also see from the figure above that if the government instead decided to auction off the 20 emissions permits the market clearing price would be \$10 per permit and result in \$200 of revenue. Since we assume that the government balances its fiscal budget, it would therefore need to reduce labor taxes by a total of \$200. Given the information that in order to collect \$1 of taxes from labor it costs the economy \$1.40, by reducing the total amount of labor tax collected by \$200 actually benefits the economy by \$280 resulting in a recycling effect (RE) of \$80.

Given that \$10 of welfare are lost for every ton of abatement we can calculate the tax interaction effect as $10 \cdot (\$-10) = \$-100)$. We also calculate the Pigovian Effect as the total reduction in damages from 0 tons of abatement to 10 tons of abatement as the area $(ABCD)$ in the figure above. Thus the PE is \$200.

The net effect, or total surplus would then be $\$80 - \$100 + \$200 = \$180$.

Chapter 14 Solutions

1. We rewrite Eq.(14.16) for two firms and multiple receptors beginning by simply rewriting a simplified version of Eq.(14.22) in the text and solve for one of the prices.

$$
\begin{aligned}
\text{Firm 1:}\quad \mathrm{MC}_1(e_1) &= -\sum_{j=1}^{J} a_{1j}\pi_j \\
\Longrightarrow -\pi_j &= \frac{\mathrm{MC}_1(e_1) + \sum_{k=1}^{K} a_{1k}\pi_k}{a_{1j}} \quad \text{for all } j \neq k \\
\Longrightarrow \pi_j &= \frac{\mathrm{MS}_1(e_1) - \sum_{k=1}^{K} a_{1k}\pi_k}{a_{1j}} \quad \text{for all } j \neq k \\
\text{Firm 2:}\quad \mathrm{MC}_2(e_2) &= -\sum_{j=1}^{J} a_{2j}\pi_j \\
\Longrightarrow -\pi_j &= \frac{\mathrm{MC}_2(e_2) + \sum_{k=1}^{K} a_{2k}\pi_k}{a_{2j}} \quad \text{for all } j \neq k \\
\Longrightarrow \pi_j &= \frac{\mathrm{MS}_2(e_2) - \sum_{k=1}^{K} a_{2k}\pi_k}{a_{2j}} \quad \text{for all } j \neq k
\end{aligned}
$$

If we consider the simplified case of 2 firms and 2 receptors we can easily see how we can begin so solve these systems of equations and arrive at an equivalent equation for Eq.(14.16) in the text:

$$
\begin{aligned}
\pi_1 = \frac{\mathrm{MS}_1(e_1) - a_{12}\pi_2}{a_{11}} &= \frac{\mathrm{MS}_2(e_2) - a_{22}\pi_2}{a_{21}} \\
a_{21}\left(\mathrm{MS}_1(e_1) - a_{12}\pi_2\right) &= a_{11}\left(\mathrm{MS}_2(e_2) - a_{22}\pi_2\right) \\
a_{11}a_{22}\pi_2 - a_{21}a_{12}\pi_2 &= a_{11}\mathrm{MS}_2(e_2) - a_{21}\mathrm{MS}_1(e_1) \\
\pi_2 &= \frac{a_{11}\mathrm{MS}_2(e_2) - a_{21}\mathrm{MS}_1(e_1)}{a_{11}a_{22} - a_{21}a_{12}} \\
\Longrightarrow \quad \pi_1 &= \frac{a_{12}\mathrm{MS}_2(e_2) - a_{22}\mathrm{MS}_1(e_1)}{a_{12}a_{21} - a_{22}a_{11}}
\end{aligned}
$$

---

2. Pollution at receptor j resulting from one unit of emissions at source i is described by the transfer coefficient a_{ij}. An ambient differentiated permit l_i^j allows the holder to produce a_{ij} units of pollution at receptor j. If the holder is source k and the transfer coefficient relating emissions at k to pollution at j is a_{kj}, then the permit allows for emissions at k equal to

$$e_k = \frac{a_{ij}}{a_{kj}}$$

a. Where there is only one receptor, there are I different types of permits, one associated with each source. Allowable emissions at source k depends on the quantities of these permits the source holds:

$$a_k e_k \leq a_i l_i^1 \quad \text{for all } i$$

where l_i^1 is the number of source i permits held by k. The maximum allowable emissions are therefore defined by the *binding* permit allocation:

$$e_k = \min_i \left\{ \frac{a_i l_i^1}{a_k} \right\}$$

b. Now there are $I \cdot J$ types of permits, where J is the number of receptors. Emissions at source k are still constrained by the one that allows the least pollution from any source.

Pollution at j from a portfolio of permits for generating pollution at $j : \sum_i a_{ij} l_i^j$

In equivalent emissions at source $k : \dfrac{\sum_i a_{ij} l_i^j}{e_{kj}}$

With a similar expression for allowable emissions at each of the J receptors, allowable emissions at k are given by

$$e_k = \min_j \left\{ \frac{\sum_i a_{ij} l_i^j}{a_{kj}} \right\}$$

---

3. a. $\text{TD}(s) = 0.01s$

where Total Damage is measured in £ and s is measured in grams of sulphate.

b. Given in the problem is the transfer equation:

$$s = e_E + 3e_D$$

where e_E represents tons of sulfur emitted in England, and e_D represents tons of sulfur emitted in Denmark. Consistent with the notation in the book, the transfer coefficients are

$$a_E = 1 \text{ and } a_D = 3$$

c. The identifying condition to find the efficient amount of emissions from England and Denmark is where each country sets the marginal savings from emissions equal to the marginal damage (in Sweden) from their emissions. From the transfer coefficients we know that 1 tonne of emissions from England and Denmark results in 1 and 3 grams of sulfates in Sweden respectively. Thus we can express the marginal damage function of emissions from England and Denmark in Sweden as

$$\text{MD}(e_E) = 0.01e_E$$

$\text{MD}(e_D) = 0.03e_D$

For each polluting country's marginal savings function we will use the duality of the marginal cost of abatement. We know that the marginal cost of abatement increases as a function of q, but the maximum amount of abatement is limited to the level of uncontrolled emissions e^* for each country. Thus for each country there is an upper bound on the marginal cost function. We are not told this upper bound for each country but we shall assume:

$$\text{MC}_E(q = e_E^*) = 2e_E^* = c$$

$$\text{MC}_D(q = e_D^*) = e_D^* = d$$

As shown in the figure below, we can now invert the marginal cost of abatement functions to marginal savings of emissions functions:

$$\text{MS}_E(e_E) = c - 2e_E$$

$$\text{MS}_D(e_D) = d - e_D$$

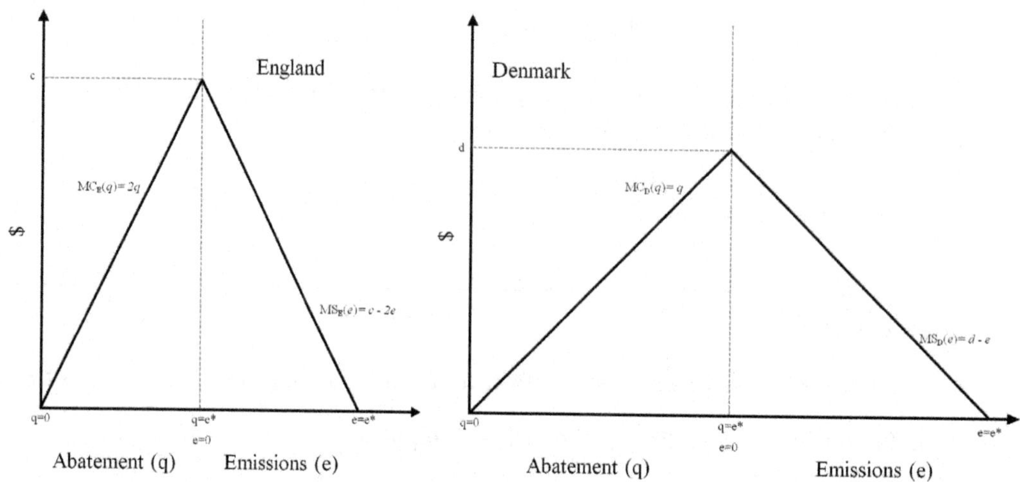

Now we set the marginal savings from each country equal to the marginal damage in Sweden from their emissions and solve for the efficient amount of emissions.

England			*Denmark*		
$\text{MS}_E(e_E)$	$\overset{set}{=}$	$\text{MD}(e_E)$	$MS_D(e_D)$	$\overset{set}{=}$	$\text{MD}(e_D)$
$c - 2e_E$	$=$	$0.01e_E$	$d - e_D$	$=$	$0.03e_D$
$\Rightarrow e_E'$	$=$	$\dfrac{c}{2.01}$	$\Rightarrow e_D'$	$=$	$\dfrac{d}{1.03}$

From these results we see that the resulting level of pollution from the emissions of these two countries would be

$$s' = \frac{c}{2.01} + 3 \cdot \left(\frac{d}{1.03}\right)$$

To find the total damage to Sweden from this level of pollution we will derive the antiderivative of the marginal damage function and assume there are no fixed damages:

$$\text{MD}(s) = [\text{TD}(s)]' \quad \Longrightarrow \text{TD}(s) = 0.005s^2$$

Thus the total damage from the efficient level of emissions would be

$$\text{TD}(s') = 0.005\left(\frac{c}{2.01} + 3 \cdot \left(\frac{d}{1.03}\right)\right)^2$$

We can also find the total control costs in the same way, with the assumption that there are no fixed control costs:

$$\textit{England}: \quad \text{MC}_E(q_E) = [\text{TC}_E(q_E)]' \quad \Longrightarrow \text{TC}_E(q_E) = q_E^2$$

$$\textit{Denmark}: \quad \text{MC}_D(q_D) = [\text{TC}_D(q_D)]' \quad \Longrightarrow \text{TC}_D(q_D) = \tfrac{1}{2}q_D^2$$

Therefore the total cost of controlling emissions from England and Denmark is

$$\begin{aligned} \text{TC}(q_E + q_D) &= q_E^2 + \tfrac{1}{2}q_D^2 \\ &= \left(\tfrac{1}{2}c - \tfrac{1}{2.01}c\right)^2 + \tfrac{1}{2}\left(d - \tfrac{1}{1.03}d\right)^2 \end{aligned}$$

d. The goal is to achieve $q_E + q_D = 12$ with minimum cost. Note: This is different from the fully optimal pollution regulation. We know cost is minimized where the marginal control costs are equal in the two countries such that $q_D = 2q_E$

Substituting the second equation into the first equation, we find that

$$q''_D = 8 \qquad q''_E = 4$$

e. Now we still want to reduce total emissions between the two countries by 12 tons, but to do so in a way that accounts for the different transfer coefficients. The logic is that reductions in Denmark are more valuable to the Swedes than reductions in England because Denmark is so much closer. This would suggest equalizing the *marginal costs of reducing sulfate deposits in Sweden.* As discussed in the text, this is the marginal cost of reducing emissions weighted by the transfer coefficient.

$$\frac{2q_E}{1} = \frac{q_D}{3}$$

Combine this condition with the target reduction in total emissions and substitute as before:

$$q_E + q_D = 12$$

$$12 = \tfrac{1}{6}q_D + q_D \quad \Longrightarrow \quad q'''_D = 10\tfrac{2}{7}$$

4. a. Transfer coefficient (Autos): $a_A = 2$
Transfer coefficient (Mill): $a_M = 1$

b. The total control cost function is defined as the sum of total cost function for controlling auto emissions and the total cost function for controlling mill emissions from the uncontrolled level of emissions as follows:

$$\begin{aligned} \mathrm{TC}(q) &= \mathrm{TC}(q_a) + \mathrm{TC}(q_m) \\ &= q_a^2 + q_m^2 \\ \Rightarrow \mathrm{TC}(e) &= (10 - e_a)^2 + (4 - e_m)^2 \end{aligned}$$

c. We know that each unit of auto emissions (e_a) results in 2 units of pollution downtown, thus if we know the level of p_a then we must divide by one half to get the level of auto emissions, i.e., $e_a = \frac{1}{2}p_a$

We also know that each unit of mill emissions (e_a) results in 1 unit of pollution downtown, i.e. $e_m = p_m$

Substituting these identities into the TC(e) function above we will have the total control cost as a function of p:

$\mathrm{TC}(p) = (10 - \frac{1}{2}p_a)^2 + (4 - p_m)^2$

d. $\mathrm{MD}(p) \quad = \left[\mathrm{TD}(p)\right]' \quad = \left[\frac{1}{2}p^2\right]' \quad = p$

e. To find the marginal damage from emissions (e), we need to split up the sources of emissions since each source has a different impact on the damage:

$\mathrm{MD}(e) = \left[\mathrm{TD}(e)\right]' = \left[\frac{1}{2}(2e_a + e_m)^2\right]'$

At this point we will take partial derivatives to determine the marginal damage caused my each source of emissions holding the emissions of the other source constant:

Autos	*Mill*
$\mathrm{MD}_a(e_a) = \dfrac{\partial \mathrm{TD}(e)}{\partial e_a}$	$\mathrm{MD}_m(e_m) = \dfrac{\partial \mathrm{TD}(e)}{\partial e_a}$
$= 4e_a + 2e_m$	$= 2e_a + e_m$

f. The two efficiency (one for each source) conditions are where MS(e) = MD(e), recall that MC(e) = −MS(e):

Autos	*Mill*
$\mathrm{MS}(e_a) \overset{set}{=} \mathrm{MD}_a(e_a)$	$\mathrm{MS}(e_m) \overset{set}{=} \mathrm{MD}_m(e_m)$

g. To find the efficient levels of emissions for the two sources, we need to determine the marginal savings functions. These we can derive from the total cost function we found in part (b).

Autos	*Mill*
$\text{MS}(e_a) = -[\text{TC}(e_a)]' = -[(10-e_a)^2]' = 20-2e_a$	$\text{MS}(e_m) = -[\text{TC}(e_m)]' = -[(4-e_m)^2]' = 8-2e_m$

$$\begin{aligned}\text{MS}(e_a) &= -[\text{TC}(e_a)]' \\ &= -[(10-e_a)^2]' \\ &= 20-2e_a\end{aligned} \qquad \begin{aligned}\text{MS}(e_m) &= -[\text{TC}(e_m)]' \\ &= -[(4-e_m)^2]' \\ &= 8-2e_m\end{aligned}$$

We can use the identifying efficiency conditions in part (f) to solve for the efficient levels of emissions from each source as a system of two equations and two unknowns. We will solve for e_m^* as a function of e_a^* from the *Autos* identifying condition in part (f) and then use that to solve for the numerical value of e_a^* in the *Mill*: identifying condition from part (f).

$$\begin{aligned}\text{MS}(e_a) &\overset{set}{=} \text{MD}_a(e_a) \\ 20-2e_a^* &= 4e_a^*+2e_m^* \\ \Rightarrow e_m^* &= 10-3e_a^*\end{aligned}$$

$$\begin{aligned}\text{MS}(e_m) &\overset{set}{=} \text{MD}_m(e_m) \\ 8-2e_m^* &= 2e_a^*+e_m^* \\ 8-2(10-3e_a^*) &= 2e_a^*+(10-3e_a^*) \\ \Rightarrow e_a^* &= 3\tfrac{1}{7} \\ \Rightarrow e_m^* &= \tfrac{4}{7}\end{aligned}$$

---

5. The stock of pollutant s at any time (t) as a continuous function of t can be given as the solution to the differential equation $\frac{ds}{dt} = -ks + \epsilon$ where k is the rate of decay $(0 < k < 1)$ and ϵ is the constant rate of emissions:

   $\text{S}(t) = \text{S}(0)e^{-kt} + \frac{\epsilon}{k}$

   where S(0) is the initial starting stock. We can rearrange the constant decay rate to a persistence rate δ (or the rate at which the stock is retained in the atmosphere) by the identity $\delta = \frac{1}{1+k}$.

   We can define the net costs of pollution and emissions as the discounted (integral) sum of all the damages that result from the stock of pollution and the discounted (integral) sum of all the costs of the emissions:

$$\begin{aligned}\text{NC} &= \int_{t=1}^{\infty} e^{-rt}\left\{\text{D}(\text{S}(t)) + \text{C}(\epsilon)\right\}dt \\ &= \int_{t=1}^{\infty} e^{-rt}\left\{\text{D}(\text{S}(0)e^{-kt}+\frac{\epsilon}{k})\right\}dt + \int_{t=1}^{\infty} e^{-rt}\left\{\text{C}(\epsilon)\right\}dt\end{aligned}$$

   where r is the continuous time discount rate. Taking the derivative of NC with respect to ϵ and setting it equal to zero we can find the efficient rate of emissions, i.e. our objective is to minimize net costs.

$$
\begin{aligned}
\frac{d\text{NC}}{d\epsilon} &= \frac{d\left[\int_{t=1}^{\infty} e^{-rt}\left\{\text{D}(\text{S}(0)e^{-kt}+\frac{\epsilon}{k})\right\}dt+\int_{t=1}^{\infty} e^{-rt}\left\{\text{C}(\epsilon)\right\}dt\right]}{d\epsilon} \\
&= \frac{d\left[\int_{t=1}^{\infty} e^{-rt}\left\{\text{D}(\text{S}(0)e^{-kt}+\frac{\epsilon}{k})\right\}dt\right]}{d\epsilon}+\frac{d\left[\int_{t=1}^{\infty} e^{-rt}\left\{\text{C}(\epsilon)\right\}dt\right]}{d\epsilon} \\
&= \int_{t=1}^{\infty} e^{-rt}\left\{\frac{\partial \text{D}(\text{S}(t))}{\partial s(t)}\cdot\frac{d\text{S}(t)}{d\epsilon}\right\}dt+\int_{t=1}^{\infty} e^{-rt}\left\{\frac{d\text{C}(\epsilon)}{d\epsilon}\right\}dt \\
&= \int_{t=1}^{\infty} e^{-rt}\left\{\text{MD}(\text{S}(t))\cdot\frac{1}{k}\right\}dt+\int_{t=1}^{\infty} e^{-rt}\left\{\text{MC}(\epsilon)\right\}dt \\
&= \frac{1}{k}\cdot\int_{t=1}^{\infty} e^{-rt}\left\{\text{MD}(\text{S}(t))\right\}dt+\frac{1}{r}\cdot\left\{\text{MC}(\epsilon)\right\} \qquad \stackrel{set}{=} 0 \\
&\Rightarrow\ \frac{1}{r}\text{MS}(\epsilon)=\frac{1}{k}\cdot\int_{t=1}^{\infty} e^{-rt}\text{MD}(\text{S}(t))\,dt
\end{aligned}
$$

Thus we should set the constant emissions rate right now such that all the discounted marginal savings for emissions is equal to the discounted (integral) sum of all the marginal damage multiplied by $^1/_k$ that will result. The main difference between this and the discrete time version is the $^1/_r$ on the left-hand side. This arises from the fact that a marginal change in the constant emissions rate yields a change in marginal savings in perpetuity. Unlike the text, though, we are not only setting the emissions in period 1 now, but a constant continuous emissions rate now and into the perpetual future.

A second way of interpreting the efficient balance between emissions and a stock pollutant is to treat it as an optimal control problem

$$\min \text{ Net Cost} = \int_{t=1}^{\infty} e^{-rt}\left\{\text{D}(\text{S}(t))+\text{C}(\epsilon)\right\}dt$$

subject to the law of motion $\dot{\text{S}} = -k\text{S}(t)+\epsilon$ where $\text{S}(t)$ is the state variable, and ϵ is the control variable.

We can state the Hamiltonian as

$$
\begin{aligned}
\mathscr{H} &= e^{-rt}\left(\text{D}(\text{S}(t))+\text{C}(\epsilon)\right)-\lambda(-k\text{S}(t)+\epsilon) \\
\mathscr{H}_{\epsilon} &= \text{MC}(\epsilon)\cdot e^{-rt}-\lambda=0 \\
\mathscr{H}_{S} &= \text{MD}\cdot e^{-rt}+\lambda k=\dot{\lambda}
\end{aligned}
$$

after substitution and rearranging the terms we find that, where $\dot{\epsilon}=0$,

$$\text{MS} = \frac{\text{MD}}{r+k}$$

which implies larger current MD when either discount rate (r or k) is higher.

6. a. Remaining faithful to the notation in the text, the transfer coefficients given in the problem are

   $a_1 = \frac{1}{2} \qquad a_2 = 1$

   b. We know that, after trading, the marginal savings from emissions for the two firms will be equal. We also know that the sum of emissions between the two firms must equal the total number of permits. This gives us two equations in two unknowns:

   $(i) \quad 10 - 2e_1 = 10 - 2e_2$

   $(ii) \quad e_1 + e_2 = 6$

   From the first equation, we see that $e_1 = e_2$; substituting this into the second equation, we arrive at the solution:

   $e_1^* = e_2^* = 3$

   The price of permits in equilibrium is the level of marginal savings for both firms:

   $P(\text{emissions permit}) = 10 - 2(3) = \$4.00$

   c. The solution to the ambient pollution permit problem is characterized by the equalization across firms of marginal savings from emissions *normalized by the transfer coefficients,* which represents marginal savings from generating a unit of ambient pollution:

   $(i) \quad \frac{10-2e_1}{\frac{1}{2}} = 10 - 2e_2$

   From the information in the question the ambient pollution permit allocations must sum to 4. The number of permits needed by firm 1 to emit emissions level e_1 is $\frac{1}{2}e_1$, while the number of ambient permits needed by firm 2 is e_2. From this information we arrive at our second equation:

   $(ii) \quad \frac{1}{2}e_1 + e_2 = 4$

   Solving equations (i) and (ii) above, we find that firm 1 will emit $e_1^* = 3\frac{3}{5}$ and firm 2 will emit $e_2^* = 2\frac{1}{5}$

   The price of an ambient pollution permit in equilibrium is given by the level of marginal savings from ambient pollution generation for both firms:

   $P(\text{ambient pollution permit}) = \frac{10-2e_1^*}{\frac{1}{2}} = 10 - 2(e_2^*) = \$5.60$

---

7. The optimal CO_2 emission fee should be equal to the marginal damage of emitting one unit of CO_2. We are told that the marginal damage of one unit of CO_2 is \$1 per year. If we can find out how much one unit of CO_2 remains in the atmosphere each year until it is gone, we can derive the discounted sum of all marginal damage from one unit of CO_2. This number should then be the optimal, or Pigovian, fee.

   Given that the persistence rate (δ) is (1-0.01) = 0.99, we know that the sum of the discounted marginal damage from one unit of CO_2 is

$$\begin{aligned}
\text{MD}_{\text{CO}_2} &= \sum_{t=0}^{\infty} \$1 \cdot \left(\frac{\delta^t}{(1+r)^t}\right) \\
&= \$1 + \$1 \cdot \left(\frac{0.99}{(1.03)}\right) + \$1 \cdot \left(\frac{0.99^2}{(1.03)^2}\right) + \$1 \cdot \left(\frac{0.99^3}{(1.03)^2}\right) + \ldots \\
&= \frac{\$1}{1 - \dfrac{0.99}{1.03}} \\
&= \$25.75
\end{aligned}$$

---

8. a. See the figure below for the plot of the stock remaining from the emission of one ton of carbon dioxide (CO_2) and one ton of methane (CH_4).

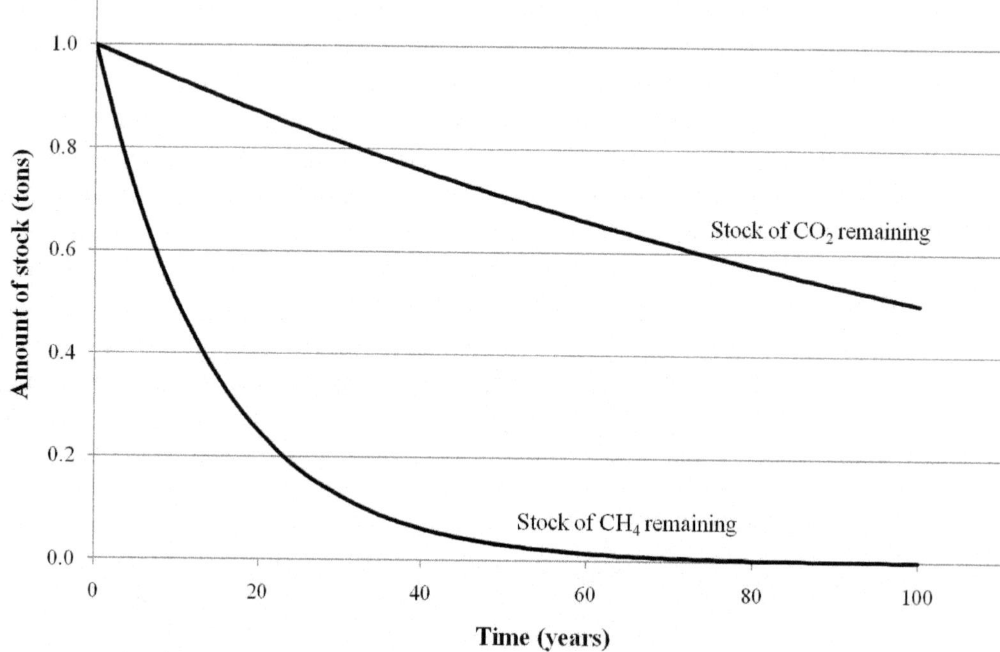

This graph was derived using the hint in the question. Since we know

$\text{stock\_remaining}_{\text{CO}_2}(t) = s_0 e^{k_{\text{CO}_2} t}$

we can solve for the decay rate k_{CO_2} by setting $0.5 = e^{k_{\text{CO}_2} 100}$ and solving. Thus we find that $k_{\text{CO}_2} = -6.9315 \times 10^{-3}$.

Using a similar logic, we can find the decay rate for CH_4 by setting $0.5 = e^{k_{\text{CH}_4} 10}$ and find that $k_{\text{CH}_4} = -6.9315 \times 10^{-2}$.

b. We begin by recognizing that the marginal damage of CO_2 = \$1 per ton per year implies that the marginal damage of CH_4 = \$25 per ton per year. Thus the discounted sum (integral) of all the marginal damage for CO_2 and CH_4 from now into the infinite future is given by

$$\begin{aligned}
\mathrm{MD}_{\mathrm{CO}_2} &= \$1 \int_0^{\infty} e^{(k_{\mathrm{CO}_2}-r)t} dt \\
&= \frac{\$1}{(k_{\mathrm{CO}_2}-r)} \cdot e^{(k_{\mathrm{CO}_2}-r)t} \Big|_{t=0}^{t=\infty} \\
&= \$27.08
\end{aligned}$$

$$\begin{aligned}
\mathrm{MD}_{\mathrm{CH}_4} &= \$25 \int_0^{\infty} e^{(k_{\mathrm{CH}_4}-r)t} dt \\
&= \frac{\$1}{(k_{\mathrm{CH}_4}-r)} \cdot e^{(k_{\mathrm{CH}_4}-r)t} \Big|_{t=0}^{t=\infty} \\
&= \$251.72
\end{aligned}$$

Therefore that ratio of the tax on methane over the tax on carbon dioxide should be $\frac{\$251.72}{\$27.08} \approx 9.3{:}1$

c. (i) If we consider only a 10-year horizon, then having reevaluated the integrals above from $t = 0$ to $t = 10$ we find that $\mathrm{MD}_{\mathrm{CO}_2} = \$8.36$ and $\mathrm{MD}_{\mathrm{CH}_4} = \$158.48$ with the ratio of the two taxes is approximately 19:1.

   (ii) If we now consider a 100-year horizon, we re-evaluate the integrals above from $t = 0$ to $t = 100$ and find that $\mathrm{MD}_{\mathrm{CO}_2} = \$26.40$ and $\mathrm{MD}_{\mathrm{CH}_4} = \$251.71$, and that the ratio of the two taxes is much closer to the infinite time horizon, being approximately 9.5:1.

d. If we now go back to the infinite time horizon for estimating damages but use a lower discount rate of 1% (by reevaluating the integrals in part (b) where $r = 0.01$) we find that $\mathrm{MD}_{\mathrm{CO}_2} = \$59.06$ and $\mathrm{MD}_{\mathrm{CH}_4} = \$315.20$, and that the ratio of the two taxes is much closer to the infinite time horizon, being approximately 5.3:1.

e. Comparing our answers from parts (c) and (d) we see that the way which we relatively evaluate the damage that occurs from methane compared to the damage from carbon dioxide depends, quite critically, on the discount rate. While under the Kyoto protocol we might evaluate the damage from methane to be about 10 times greater than that of carbon dioxide, we see that by using a small change in discount rate and an infinite time horizon the relative damage might be closer to only half as much as we originally thought. Such differences in how we think about the relative damage of methane versus carbon dioxide could have large and serious policy implications for different nations in negotiating international environmental agreements.

Chapter 15 Solutions

1. As shown in the figure below, there are the four possible marginal savings functions MS_1, MS_2, MS_3, MS_4. In the figure the hybrid fee and subsidy are chosen to minimize expected deadweight loss from emissions. We suppose each of the four marginal savings curves is equally likely. To minimize expected deadweight loss, the regulator would want to choose a subsidy level in-between MS_1 and MS_2 and a fee level in-between MS_3 and MS_4. The optimal combination would minimize the sum of the four possible deadweight loss areas $\{A, B, C, D\}$.

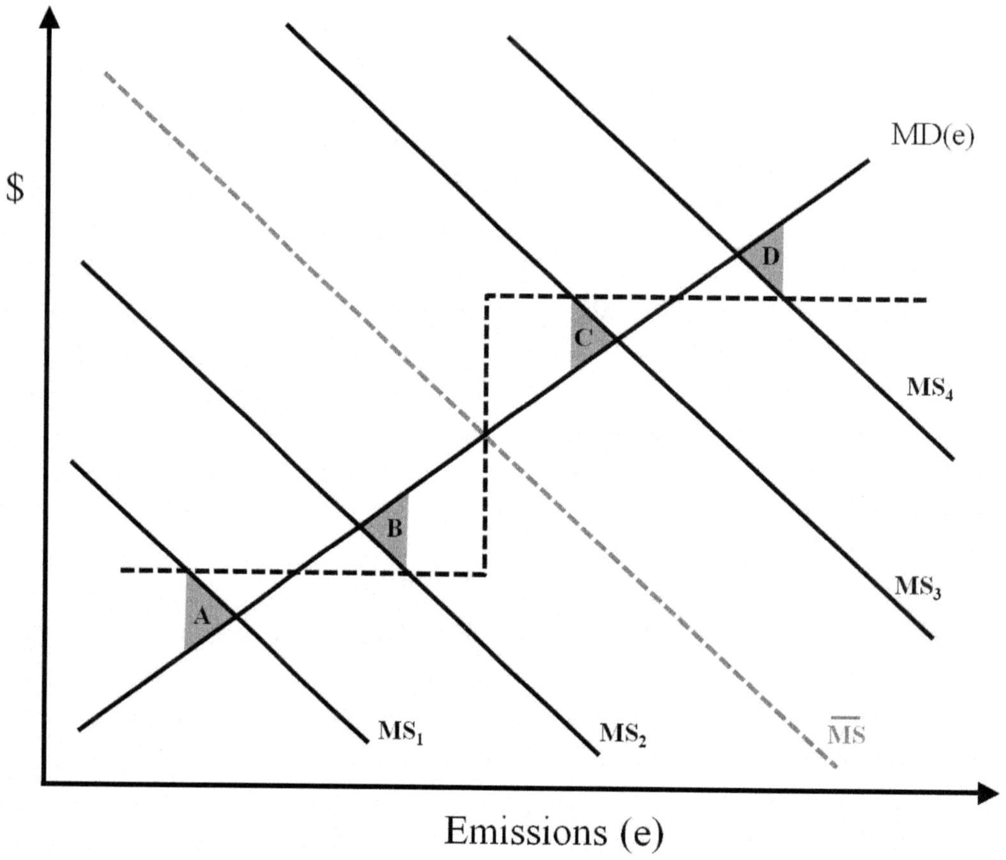

2. For this question we shall reduce our attention to comparing the outcomes of the coin flip for a firm that has either a *low-* or *high*-marginal-savings function. In the figure below we show that the loss from the outcome if the firm lies (saying MS is *high* when is it in fact *low*) is larger than potential savings - thus it would appear that the firm has an incentive to tell the truth. To explain: Suppose a firm actually has a low-cost marginal-savings function but lies and states that their MS is high. If the outcome of the regulators coin flip is permits, then the shaded area labeled "gain" is a surplus to the firm as compared to if they had told the truth. However, if the coin-flip outcome is a fee system, then the firm loses the shaded area labeled "loss" as compared to if it had told the truth.

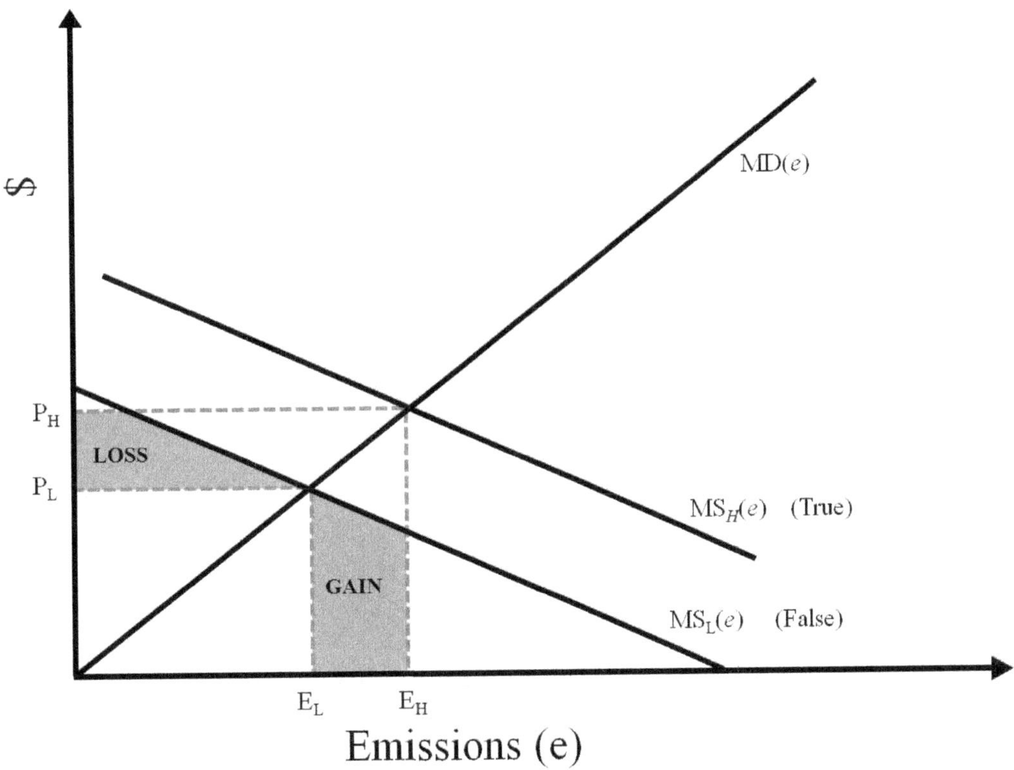

We could depict the counterexample to the one above, where we can consider the case if the firm is actually a high-marginal-savings emitter, but it lies and states it is a low-marginal-cost emitter. Then the potential "gain" might be smaller than the "loss." We quickly realize that the outcome of whether or not the firm has the incentive to tell the truth in this coin-flip regulatory design depends on whether or not the firm has actually high or low marginal savings and on how steep the slopes of the marginal-savings functions are and the slope of the marginal-damage function.

3. a. Substituting the identity $q = 2 - e$ into the total cost function, we find

$$\text{TC} = (3 + r)(2 - e)^2$$

The figure below is the graph of total cost for the two levels of r. Note: Emissions will not exceed 2, since the amount of uncontrolled emissions is only 2.

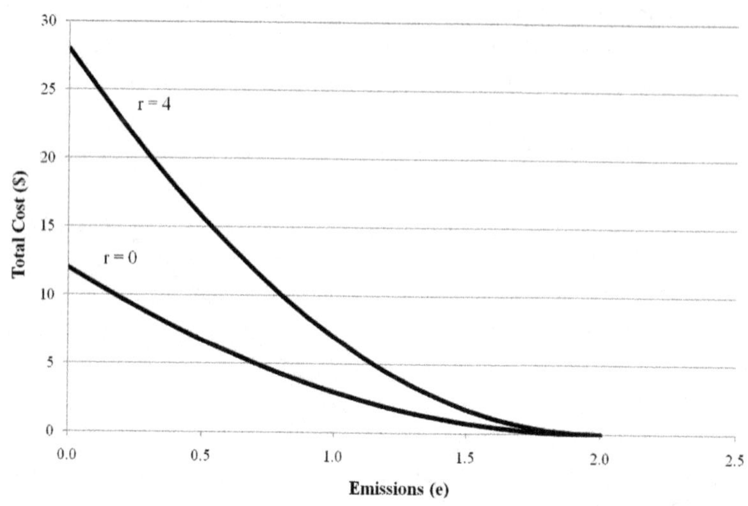

b. From the total cost function (of e) we derive the marginal savings function:

$$\begin{aligned} \text{MS}(e) &= -[\text{TC}(e)]' \\ &= -[(3+r)(2-e)^2]' \\ &= 2(3+r)(2-e) \end{aligned}$$

$$\begin{aligned} \text{MS}(e|r=0) &= 12 - 6e \\ \text{MS}(e|r=4) &= 28 - 14e \end{aligned}$$

The figure below shows the graph of the marginal damage function, the two marginal savings functions, and the average marginal savings function.

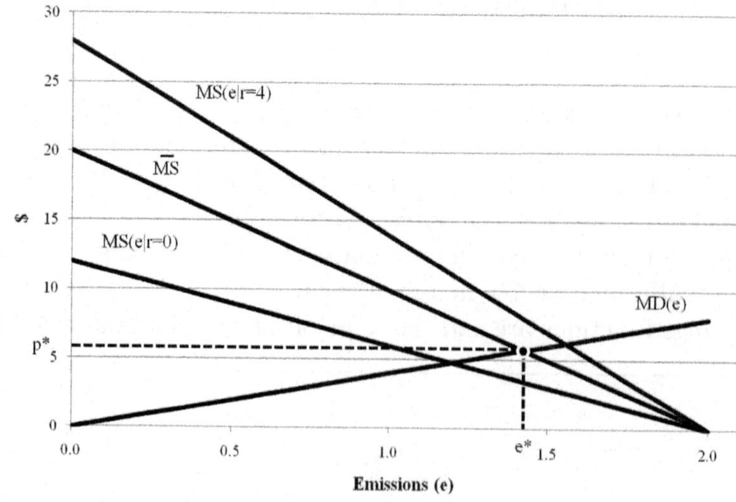

c. The level of emissions fee or number of emissions permits that should be chosen, given the level of r is not known is shown above. To find the level of e^* and p^* we set $\overline{\text{MS}} = \text{MD}(e)$

$$\begin{aligned} \overline{\text{MS}} &\overset{set}{=} \text{MD}(e) \\ 20 - 10e &= 4e \\ \Rightarrow e^* &= 1\tfrac{3}{7} \\ \Rightarrow p^* &= 5\tfrac{5}{7} \end{aligned}$$

d. The dead weight loss (DWL) associated with the question is shown in the figure below - the graph of the relevant region has been magnified. It appears that the DWL associated with the fee p^* is less than the DWL associated with e^*.

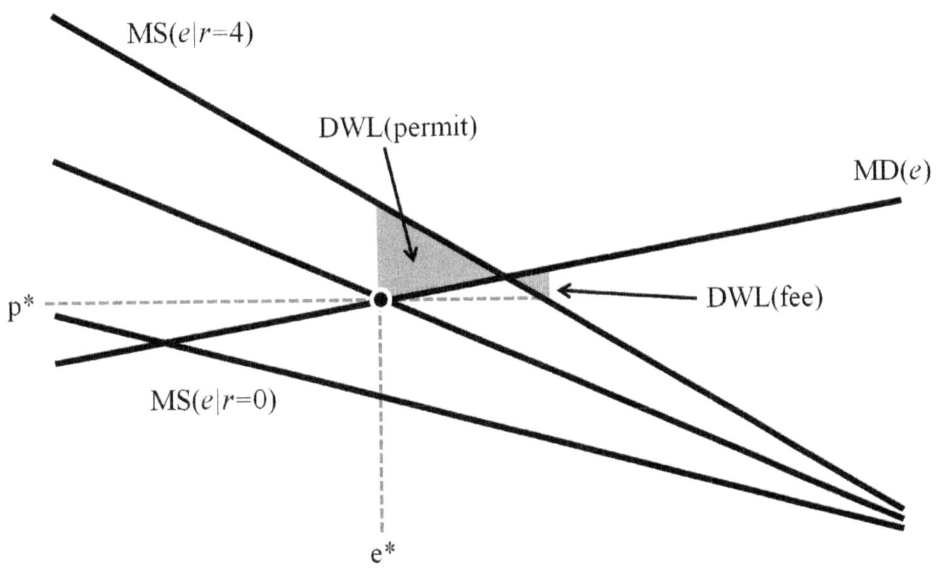

4. a. There are four possible combinations of θ_1 and θ_2: $(\theta_1, \theta_2) =$

I. (1,1) II. (1,2) III. (2,1) IV. (2,2)

We will present the optimality conditions for each of these cases below by first setting each firms marginal savings functions equal to each other to find the efficient identity condition, then solve for the optimal level of emissions using the marginal damage function, i.e.:

$$\begin{aligned} (i) \quad \text{MS}_1 &= \text{MS}_2 \\ (ii) \quad \text{MS}_i &= \text{MD} \end{aligned}$$

I. $\theta_1 = 1 \quad \theta_2 = 1$

$$\begin{aligned} (i) \qquad 1 - e_1 &\overset{set}{=} 1 - e_2 \\ \Rightarrow e_1 &= e_2 \\ (ii) \qquad 1 - e_1 &\overset{set}{=} e_1 + e_1 \\ \Rightarrow e_1^*(1,1) &= \tfrac{1}{3} \\ \Rightarrow e_2^*(1,1) &= \tfrac{1}{3} \end{aligned}$$

II. $\theta_1 = 1 \quad \theta_2 = 2$

$$\begin{aligned} (i) \qquad 1 - e_1 &\overset{set}{=} 1 - 2e_2 \\ \Rightarrow e_1 &= 2e_2 \\ (ii) \qquad 1 - e_1 &\overset{set}{=} e_1 + \tfrac{1}{2}e_1 \\ \Rightarrow e_1^*(1,1) &= \tfrac{2}{5} \\ \Rightarrow e_2^*(1,1) &= \tfrac{1}{5} \end{aligned}$$

III. $\theta_1 = 2 \quad \theta_2 = 1$ By the symmetry between II and III, we can see that

$e_1^*(2,1) = \frac{2}{5}$

$e_2^*(2,1) = \frac{2}{5}$

IV. $\theta_1 = 2 \quad \theta_2 = 2$

$$\begin{aligned} (i) \qquad 1 - 2e_1 &\overset{set}{=} 1 - 2e_2 \\ \Rightarrow e_1 &= e_2 \\ (ii) \qquad 1 - 2e_1 &\overset{set}{=} e_1 + e_1 \\ \Rightarrow e_1^*(2,2) &= \tfrac{1}{4} \\ \Rightarrow e_2^*(2,2) &= \tfrac{1}{4} \end{aligned}$$

b. The strategy for showing that the regulation described creates the incentive for each firm to truthfully reveal their value of θ and to emit the efficient amount, e^*, is as follows:

(i) Show that e_i^* (from part a.) maximizes savings minus taxes $(S_i - T_i)$ when θ_i has been revealed truthfully.

(ii) Show that maximum $(S_i - T_i)$ is greater when reporting θ_i truthfully.

(i) The firm's objective is to maximize the difference between savings from emissions, S_1, and T_1, the amount charged by the regulator:

$$S_1 - T_1 = S_1(e_1, \theta_1) - D[e_1 + e_2^*(\widehat{\theta})] + S_2[e_2^*(\widehat{\theta}), \widehat{\theta}_2]$$

With the given functional forms for D and S, this becomes

$$S_1 - T_1 = 2 - \frac{(1 - \theta_1 e_1)^2}{2\theta_1} - \frac{[e_1 + e_2^*(\widehat{\theta})]^2}{2} - \frac{[1 - \widehat{\theta}_2 e_2^*(\widehat{\theta})]^2}{2\widehat{\theta}_2}$$

Throughout, $\widehat{\theta}$ will represent reported values, θ will represent actual values. e^* will represent optimal emissions found in part (a) and e will represent chosen emissions.

It is necessary to do this for firm 1 only, since the two firms are identical. First consider the options of firm 1, conditional on the information that firm 2 is reporting $\widehat{\theta_2} = 1$. Firm 1 could report $\widehat{\theta_1} = 1$:

$\widehat{\theta} = (1, 1) \longrightarrow e^* = (\frac{1}{3}, \frac{1}{3})$ from part (a)

$$\begin{aligned}[S_1 - T_1 \mid \widehat{\theta} = (1,1)] &= 2 - \frac{(1-\theta_1 e_1)^2}{2\theta_1} - \frac{(e_1 + \frac{1}{3})}{2} - \frac{[1-(1)\frac{1}{3}]^2}{2(1)} \\ &= 2 - \tfrac{4}{18} - \frac{(1-\theta_1 e_1)^2}{2\theta_1} - \frac{(e_1 + \frac{1}{3})}{2} \\ &= 1\tfrac{7}{9} - \frac{(1-\theta_1 e_1)^2}{2\theta_1} - \frac{(e_1 + \frac{1}{3})}{2}\end{aligned}$$

Once established, the firm chooses e_1, actual emissions, to maximize this expression:

Max where $1 - \theta_1 e_1 = e_1 + \frac{1}{3}$

The solution depends on the true value of θ_1 :

$\theta_1 = 1 \longrightarrow \frac{2}{3} = 2e_1 \longrightarrow e_1 = \frac{1}{3}\ (= e_1^*)$

$\theta_1 = 2 \longrightarrow \frac{2}{3} = 3e_1 \longrightarrow e_1 = \frac{2}{9}\ (\neq e_1^*)$

Alternatively, the firm can report $\widehat{\theta_1} = 2$.

$\widehat{\theta} = (2, 1) \longrightarrow e^* = (\frac{1}{5}, \frac{2}{5})$ from part (a)

$$\begin{aligned}[S_1 - T_1 \mid \widehat{\theta} = (2,1)] &= 2 - \frac{(1-\theta_1 e_1)^2}{2\theta_1} - \frac{(e_1 + \frac{2}{5})}{2} - \frac{[1-(1)\frac{2}{5}]^2}{2(1)} \\ &= 2 - \tfrac{9}{50} - \frac{(1-\theta_1 e_1)^2}{2\theta_1} - \frac{(e_1 + \frac{2}{5})}{2} \\ &= 1\tfrac{41}{50} - \frac{(1-\theta_1 e_1)^2}{2\theta_1} - \frac{(e_1 + \frac{2}{5})}{2}\end{aligned}$$

Max where $1 - \theta_1 e_1 = e_1 + \frac{2}{5}$

The solution again depends on the true value of θ_1 :

$\theta_1 = 1 \longrightarrow \frac{3}{5} = 2e_1 \longrightarrow e_1 = \frac{3}{10}\ (\neq e_1^*)$

$\theta_1 = 2 \longrightarrow \frac{3}{5} = 3e_1 \longrightarrow e_1 = \frac{1}{5}\ (= e_1^*)$

We see that *if* θ_1 has been truthfully reported, firm 1 will choose to emit e_1^* from part (a)

(ii) The second step is to show that the firm will, in fact, want to truthfully reveal θ_1. For this, it is demonstrated that $(S_1 - T_1)$ is greater when the firm tells the truth, i.e.:

(1) $[S_1 - T_1 \mid \widehat{\theta} = (1,1); \theta_1 = 1] > [(S_1 - T_1) \mid \widehat{\theta} = (2,1); \theta_1 = 1]$

(2) $[S_1 - T_1 \mid \widehat{\theta} = (2,1); \theta_1 = 2] > [(S_1 - T_1) \mid \widehat{\theta} = (1,1); \theta_1 = 2]$

Consider these in turn:

(1) $[S_1 - T_1 \mid \widehat{\theta} = (1,1); \theta_1 = 1] = 1\frac{7}{9} - \dfrac{(1-\frac{1}{3})^2}{2} - \dfrac{(\frac{1}{3}+\frac{1}{3})^2}{2}$

$= 1\frac{7}{9} - \frac{4}{18} - \frac{4}{18} = 1\frac{4}{9} \approx 1.44$

$[S_1 - T_1 \mid \widehat{\theta} = (2,1); \theta_1 = 1] = 1\frac{41}{50} - \dfrac{(1-\frac{3}{10})^2}{2} - \dfrac{(\frac{3}{10}+\frac{2}{5})^2}{2}$

$= \frac{91}{50} - \frac{49}{200} - \frac{49}{200} = 1\frac{66}{200} = 1.33$

(2) $[S_1 - T_1 \mid \widehat{\theta} = (2,1); \theta_1 = 2] = 1\frac{41}{50} - \dfrac{[1-(2)(\frac{1}{5})]^2}{2(2)} - \dfrac{(\frac{1}{5}+\frac{3}{5})^2}{2}$

$= \frac{91}{50} - \frac{9}{100} - \frac{9}{50} = \frac{155}{100} = 1.55$

$[S_1 - T_1 \mid \widehat{\theta} = (1,1); \theta_1 = 2] = 1\frac{7}{9} - \dfrac{[1-(2)(\frac{2}{9})]^2}{2(2)} - \dfrac{(\frac{2}{9}+\frac{1}{3})^2}{2}$

$= \frac{16}{9} - \frac{25}{324} - \frac{25}{162} = \frac{501}{324} = 1.547$

These are very close, but the result holds. When $\widehat{\theta_2} = 1$, is it optimal for firm one to report $\widehat{\theta_1} = 1$ when $\theta_1 = 1$, and $\widehat{\theta_1} = 2$ when $\theta_1 = 2$ Furthermore, it is subsequently optimal for firm 1 to emit e_1^* from part a. The same can be shown for the case where $\widehat{\theta_2} = 2$. The firm could report $\widehat{\theta_1} = 1:$

$\widehat{\theta} = (1,2) \longrightarrow e^* = (\frac{2}{5}, \frac{1}{5})$ from part (a).

$[S_1 - T_1 \mid \widehat{\theta} = (1,2)] = 2 - \dfrac{(1-\theta_1 e_1)^2}{2\theta_1} - \dfrac{(e_1+\frac{1}{5})^2}{2} - \dfrac{[1-(2)\frac{1}{5}]^2}{2(2)}$

$= \frac{191}{100} - \dfrac{(1-\theta_1 e_1)^2}{2\theta_1} - \dfrac{(e_1+\frac{1}{5})^2}{2}$

Max where $1 - \theta_1 e_1 = e_1 + \frac{1}{5}$

The solution again depends on the true value of θ_1:

$\theta_1 = 1 \longrightarrow \frac{4}{5} = 2e_1 \longrightarrow e_1 = \frac{2}{5}\ (= e_1^*)$

$\theta_1 = 2 \longrightarrow \frac{4}{5} = 3e_1 \longrightarrow e_1 = \frac{4}{15}\ (\neq e_1^*)$

And $\widehat{\theta_1} = 2:$

$\widehat{\theta} = (2,2) \longrightarrow e^* = (\frac{1}{4}, \frac{1}{4})$ from part (a).

$$[S_1 - T_1 \mid \widehat{\theta} = (2,2)] = 2 - \frac{(1-\theta_1 e_1)^2}{2\theta_1} - \frac{(e_1 + \frac{1}{4})^2}{2} - \frac{[1-(2)\frac{1}{4}]^2}{2(2)}$$

$$= 1\frac{15}{16} - \frac{(1-\theta_1 e_1)^2}{2\theta_1} - \frac{(e_1 + \frac{1}{4})^2}{2}$$

Max where $1 - \theta_1 e_1 = e_1 + \frac{1}{4}$

The solution again depends on the true value of θ_1 :

$\theta_1 = 1 \longrightarrow \frac{3}{4} = 2e_1 \longrightarrow e_1 = \frac{3}{8}\ (\neq e_1^*)$

$\theta_1 = 2 \longrightarrow \frac{3}{4} = 3e_1 \longrightarrow e_1 = \frac{1}{4}\ (= e_1^*)$

The conditions describing the desirability of truth-telling:

(1) $[S_1 - T_1 \mid \widehat{\theta} = (2,2); \theta_1 = 2] > [(S_1 - T_1) \mid \widehat{\theta} = (1,2); \theta_1 = 2]$

(2) $[S_1 - T_1 \mid \widehat{\theta} = (1,2); \theta_1 = 1] > [(S_1 - T_1) \mid \widehat{\theta} = (2,2); \theta_1 = 1]$

Consider these in turn:

(1) $$[S_1 - T_1 \mid \widehat{\theta} = (2,2); \theta_1 = 2] = 1\tfrac{15}{16} - \frac{[1-(2)\frac{1}{4}]^2}{2(2)} - \frac{(\frac{1}{4}+\frac{1}{4})^2}{2}$$

$$= \tfrac{31}{16} - \tfrac{1}{16} - \tfrac{1}{8} = 1.75$$

$$[S_1 - T_1 \mid \widehat{\theta} = (2,2); \theta_1 = 2] = \tfrac{191}{100} - \frac{[1-(2)\frac{4}{15}]^2}{2(2)} - \frac{(\frac{4}{15}+\frac{1}{5})^2}{2}$$

$$= \tfrac{191}{100} - \tfrac{49}{900} - \tfrac{49}{450} = 1.747$$

(2) $$[S_1 - T_1 \mid \widehat{\theta} = (1,2); \theta_1 = 1] = \tfrac{191}{100} - \frac{[1-(1)\frac{2}{5}]^2}{2(1)} - \frac{(\frac{2}{5}+\frac{1}{5})^2}{2}$$

$$= \tfrac{191}{100} - \tfrac{9}{50} - \tfrac{9}{50} = 1.55$$

$$[S_1 - T_1 \mid \widehat{\theta} = (2,2); \theta_1 = 1] = 1\tfrac{15}{16} - \frac{[1-(1)\frac{3}{8}]^2}{2(1)} - \frac{(\frac{3}{8}+\frac{1}{4})^2}{2}$$

$$= 1\tfrac{15}{16} - \tfrac{25}{128} - \tfrac{26}{128} = 1.547$$

This result is not specific to the functional forms given, but has been shown to be rather general. This is the so-called Clark–Groves mechanism.

5. a. We would expect firms to announce that that they are a low-marginal-cost emitter in order to enjoy a lower emission fee.

   b. For a reward system, a firm needs to be rewarded for admitting it is a high-marginal-cost emitter, since we know that no reward will be needed for a firm to admit it is a low-cost emitter. Consistent with the notation in the text, we need to structure the reward system such that the following conditions are satisfied:

   If the firm is high cost, then it should be cheaper for the firm to tell the truth and admit high cost, than to claim it is low cost, i.e.,

   $C_H(r_H) - R_H < C_H(r_L)$

   Also, if the firm is a low-cost emitter, then it should be cheaper for the firm to admit being a low-cost firm, than claim being a high-cost firm to get the reward, i.e.,

   $C_L(r_L) < C_L(r_H) - R_H$

   Putting these two conditions together implies

   $C_H(r_H) - C_H(r_L) < R_H < C_L(r_H) - C_L(r_L)$

   c. We see from the figure below that the benefit from lying if the firm is high-cost is the area {ABEF}, while the benefit from telling the truth if the firm is low-cost is the area {CDEF}. It appears, graphically, that {ABEF} > {CDEF}; in other words, the benefit from lying is greater than the benefit from telling the truth. It will be very difficult to find a level of reward that could induce a high-cost firm to tell the truth without providing sufficient incentives for a low-cost firm to lie. In other words, the reward for a high-cost firm to tell the truth must be greater than {ABEF}. Unfortunately, this amount is greater than the benefit for a low-cost firm to tell the truth, and the low-cost firm would have a strong incentive to lie and say it was a high-cost firm to get the reward too.

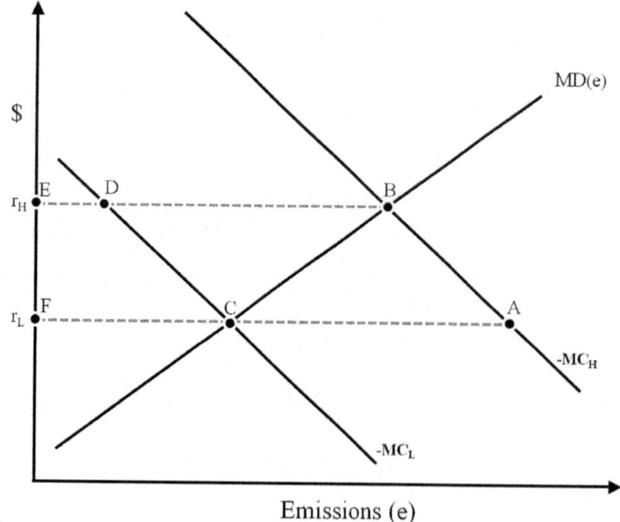

Chapter 16 Solutions

1. The logic behind such a program is that it is more costly to dispose of wastes appropriately (in compliance with the law) than in some inappropriate fashion. This potential cost savings provides an incentive for firms to secretly dispose of wastes unsafely ("midnight dumping"). This unobserved behavior by firms is a moral hazard problem. A reward scheme wherein the per unit reward, paid when appropriate disposal is undertaken, is greater than the per unit savings from dumping illegally would "fix" the incentives for firms: it is now worthwhile to dispose of wastes appropriately. For instance, particular hazardous wastes are often associated with the use of certain chemicals. One policy solution involves taxing the chemicals to reduce their use and raise revenue for the safe disposal subsidies. This is a common solution to moral hazard problems in regulation; where actions cannot be observed, it is logical to create the right incentives for firms.

   The shortcomings of such a scheme arise with unintended changes in other incentives. Especially where the reward is sizable, this may change the firms perceived marginal costs of waste *production*. Abatement of waste now carries the extra cost of the foregone reward. It is difficult to say if this will be significant or not. In addition, there is a property rights issue to consider. A scheme such as this implies that firms have the right to dispose of wastes in any fashion, and the community has to pay the firm to dispose of waste safely. A strict liability regulation, one where the penalty for illegal dumping is sufficiently high so that the firm (even if it may associate a small probability with being caught) chooses to dispose properly, is a regulatory solution where the property right is given to the community. A problem with this option is the high monitoring costs associated with even a modest probability of detection.

---

2. The plan outlined in Section II, A in the text would be difficult to implement for the regulation of air pollution by automobiles because of the large number of non-point sources (cars). However, the scheme would involve charging a fee to motorists based on the difference between the ambient levels of pollution and some "acceptable" level. We see in the chapter that this leads to the following perception of pollution costs by a single driver, driver i:

   $$C = C(e_i) + t(p - p^*)$$

   where p is the actual level of emissions and p^* is the acceptable level. Since p is a function of this driver's pollution and everyone else in the area (maybe millions of other people), this is

   $$C = C(e_i) + t(a_i e_i + \textstyle\sum_{j\neq i} a_j e_j - p^*)$$

   $$C = C(e_i) + t a_i e_i + (\text{constant})$$

   The last term is a constant since, as a function only of other drivers' behavior, it is not under the control of driver i. Note that this term could be positive or negative.

   The solution to a motorist's cost minimization problem requires

   $$-\text{MC}(e) = t a_i$$

From the text we understand that a tax set where $t = \mathrm{MD}(p^*)$ would create the incentive for optimal pollution levels by each motorist. The problem is that this requires a tax t equal to social marginal damage from pollution from driver i, but the constant represents marginal damages from all other drivers too. This could be extremely high, perhaps in the range of thousands of dollars per day per motorist. While the incentive to drive at the optimal level is ensured, this would be likely to generate strong political opposition, to say the least.

---

3. a. Adverse selection - hidden costs. The true characteristics of the firms costs are unknown to the regulator, and the incentive to the firm is to exaggerate its abatement costs. The regulator is forced to set suboptimal regulations in the presence of this imperfect information.

   b. Moral hazard - hidden actions. Motorists have no incentive to keep their automobile in compliance with the emissions standards once their vehicle passes the test. Additional regulation to monitor the emissions of cars or the maintenance of equipment may be needed, but may be cost prohibitive.

   c. Adverse selection - hidden costs. The emissions levels, how often the car is actually driven, and other characteristics of the car and/or driver are not known to the regulator. The regulator may end up paying for a lot of old vehicles that are rarely used, and thus do not contribute much to ambient pollution, while not removing clunkers owned by people who use their car a lot but do not have the resources to replace their needed vehicle with something newer and more efficient.

---

4. Emissions fees and marketable permits are mentioned together in the text as incentive-based regulatory instruments that achieve economic efficiency. But they are clearly not completely equivalent. Primary differences discussed in the text are the issues of revenue-raising vs. non-revenue-raising, payment of residual damages, and to whom property rights are granted.

   An additional issue with respect to property rights concerns the flexibility of fees relative to permits in a society where property cannot be confiscated without compensation. A system of fees implicitly grants the property right of a clean environment to members of society; the fee is the government (on behalf of the people) "selling" some of that right to polluters. The fee is under the control of the government (to the extent it can enforce the law) and can be changed relatively easily. A system of tradable permits, on the contrary, grants the right to pollute to polluters. Those who have polluted in the past may rightfully argue that if they do not initially receive their full allocation of permits, they must be compensated for the governments taking away their right. Similarly, if the government wants to reduce emissions after permits have been granted, the government has no choice but to purchase back permits and retire them.

---

5. a. When the price on emissions is zero, then the level of uncontrolled emissions is 10,000 km/year $\times$ 10 g(CO)/km = 100 kilograms/year of CO emissions per driver.

If the cost of emissions is $R10$/kilogram of CO, then the marginal cost of driving increases from $R0.3$/km to $R0.4$/km and the average driver choses to drive only 9000 km/year. Thus 90 kilograms/year of CO will be emitted by the average driver.

Since we are told that the demand function for driving is linear, we can see that if the cost of emissions is $R20$/kilogram of CO, then the marginal cost of driving increases to $R0.5$/km and the average driver will choose to drive 8000 km/year and emit 80 kilograms/year of CO. Plotting out these points and interpolating, we get the figure below.

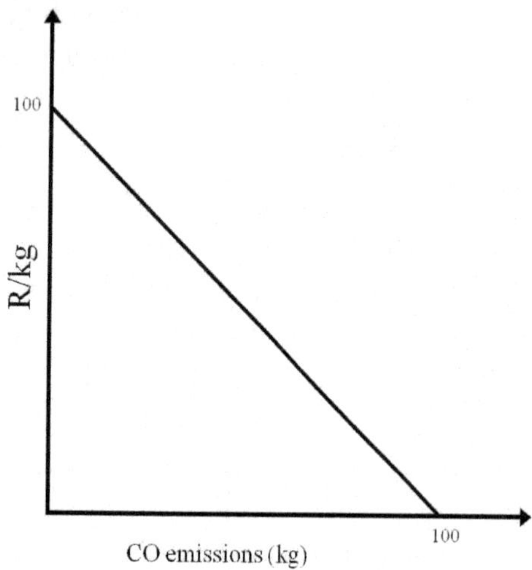

b. The figure below shows the two graphs for the question. The first is the total emissions (in kilotons) from each of the 1 million drivers. We can easily see that this graph is the aggregation of the 1 million motorists' emissions when each is charged so many Rubles per kg of emissions, i.e. at no emissions price the 1 million drivers produce 100 kg of CO/year generating in total 100 kg $\times$ 10^6 motorists $\times$ $\frac{1}{1000}$ kg/ton $\times$ $\frac{1}{1000}$ tons/kilotons = 100 kt of CO.

The second is the aggregate supply of pollution (μg/m^3) and the price in millions of Rubles. We can see how the first graph below translates into the second graph since we are told that each kiloton of CO emissions results in 1 μg/m^3 of CO pollution. Also, that an emissions charge of, say, $10R$/kg corresponds to an emissions charge of $10{\times}10^6$ R/μg/m^3, since there are $1{\times}10^6$ kilograms in 1 kiloton and 1 kiloton for 1 μg/m^3. In other words if a motorist wanted to raise the ambient pollution levels by 1 μg/m^3 they would need to emit 1 million kg of CO in so doing incur the cost of 10 million Rubles (if the price of emissions was $10R$/kg.

We see from the second graph that the efficient point S is where the marginal damage from pollution equals the marginal savings from pollution. This intersection is at a pollution level of 90 $\mu g/m^3$.

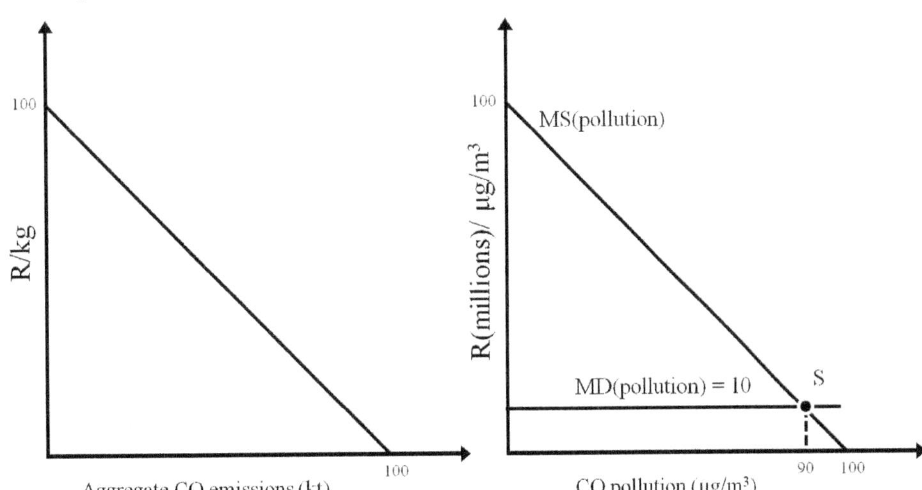

c. The efficient level of pollution S is associated with an aggregate CO emissions level of 90 kilotons, or on average, 90 kilograms of CO per car per year. If we could observe emissions from each vehicle then we would levy a fee of $R10$/kg of CO emissions.

d. Under the ambient fee system described in the text, if the ambient CO pollution exceeded 90 $\mu g/m^3$ by 1 $\mu g/m^3$ then *every* motorist would need to pay the marginal damage associated with that additional microgram of pollution, i.e., every motorist would need to pay $R10,000,000$.

e. The solution to part (d) is not tenable. Virtually no one would be able (and fewer willing!) to pay such a potentially enormous tax. The concept of the optimal ambient tax is a theoretical one. It is not a practical policy option when many polluters are involved, as with automobile emissions.

   The tax in part (c) is a little more reasonable - each motorist paying for external damage from his or her emissions. We note though that emissions from mobile sources are very difficult to observe by a regulator. The simplest solution would appear to be to take advantage of the direct relationship between km driven and kg of emissions. If the regulator can raise the marginal cost of driving by $R0.1$ per km, the marginal cost of emissions is increased by $R10$ per kg - since everyone drives the same kind of car. Furthermore, distance driven is easy to tax through gasoline.

6. a. To comply with the regulation would require the rubber duck firm to for-go savings by not polluting the water. We see that, in the absence of regulation, the firm would want to pollute up to the point where MS = 0, and would emit 10 units of pollution. Cutting back to polluting only 2 units would mean forgoing $\int_{10}^{2}(10 - e)\, de$ million dollars.

$$\begin{aligned}\int_{10}^{2}(10-e)\, de &= -\tfrac{1}{2}(10-e)^2\Big|_{e=2}^{e=10}\\ &= \left[-\tfrac{1}{2}(10-(10))^2\right] - \left[-\tfrac{1}{2}(10-(2))^2\right]\\ &= \$32 \text{ million}\end{aligned}$$

b. Given the auditing progam the firm now internalizes the cost of being audited and being caught. Instead of polluting to the point where marginal savings equals zero, it will now pollute to the point where marginal savings equals the marginal cost of being audited. We can define the expected total cost of polluting and being audited as

$$\begin{aligned}\text{TC}(e) &= \text{P}\left[\$10 \times 10^6(e-2)\right] \qquad \text{for } 2 < e \leq 10\\ &= 0.01 \cdot \left[\$10 \times 10^6(e-2)\right]\\ \Rightarrow \text{MC}(e) &= \$10,000\\ &= \$0.01 \text{ (millions)}\end{aligned}$$

We can find the optimal point of pollution where MC(e) equals MS(e):

$$\begin{aligned}\text{MC}(e) &\overset{set}{=} \text{MS}(e)\\ 0.01 &= 10 - e\\ \Rightarrow e^* &= 9.99\end{aligned}$$

---

7. Assign the following from the information in the problem:

P_g = prob. of audit with a gold star = 0.1, P_b = prob. of audit with black mark = 0.5, u = prob. of being granted a gold star when audited with a black star and found in compliance = 0.5, F_g = fine if caught out of compliance with a gold star = 50, F_b = fine if caught out of compliance with a black mark = 100, β = discount factor = 0.9

First we need to calculate the discounted expected costs for the 8 different scenarios (4 strategies times 2 initial conditions)

i. $C_{cc}(g)$: A firm endowed with a gold star and always complies. This costs k every period forever:

$$C_{cc}(g) = k + \beta k + \beta^2 k + \ldots = \frac{k}{1-\beta} = 10k$$

ii. $C_{cc}(b)$: A firm endowed with a black mark and chooses to always comply.

$C_{cc}(b) = \frac{k}{1-\beta} = 10k$

iii. $C_{nn}(b)$: A firm endowed with a black mark and chooses to never comply, but rather pay the fine when audited and caught. The probability of being audited when endowed with a black mark is given in the problem as 0.5, and the penalty is 100.

$C_{nn}(b) = 0.5(100) + \beta 0.5(100) + \beta^2 0.5(100) = \frac{50}{1-\beta} = 500$

iv. $C_{nn}(g)$: This is a very similar scenario to (iii), but because this firm is endowed with a gold star, the initial likelihood of an audit is lower at 0.1. Once caught and fined (F_g), the problem is identical to (iii):

$$\begin{aligned} C_{nn}(g) &= P_g[F_g + \beta C_{nn}(b)] + (1 - P_g)\beta C_{nn}(g) \\ &= 0.1[50 + 0.9(500)] + (0.9)^2 C_{nn}(g) \\ C_{nn}(g)(1 - 0.81) &= 5 + 45 \\ C_{nn}(g) &= 263.16 \end{aligned}$$

v. $C_{cn}(g)$: This is a strange strategy. It involves compliance when the firm has a gold star, but non-compliance when it does not. Because this firm starts with a gold star, they comply and never lose it (this is the same as $C_{cc}(g)$).

$C_{cn}(g) = \frac{k}{1-\beta} = 10k$

vi. The same strategy as (v), but this firm is endowed initially with a black mark. They would never comply, keeping the black mark forever (this is the same as $C_{nn}(b)$).

$C_{cn}(b) = \frac{50}{1-\beta} = 500$

vii. and viii. (Expected costs for C_{nc} will have to be solved together.) This is a logical strategy: comply when a black mark increases both the probability of an audit and the penalty if caught, but don't comply when a gold star makes and audit unlikely and the penalty smaller.

$C_{nc}(g) = P_g[F_g + \beta C_{nc}(b)] + (1 - P_g)\beta C_{nc}(g)$

The above says that, if audited, the firm is fined F_g and faces the (discounted) future costs of this strategy starting with a black mark. If it is not audited, the firm's expected future costs are unchanged. Rearranging yields $C_{nc}(g)$ in terms of $C_{nc}(b)$:

$$(1) \qquad C_{nc}(g) = \frac{P_g[F_g + \beta C_{nc}(b)]}{[1 - (1 - P_g)\beta]}$$

A firm using this strategy starting with a black mark will comply in the first period The probability of an audit is P_b, with a subsequent u probability of winning a gold star:

$$C_{nc}(b) = k + \beta\{P_b u C_{nc}(g) + (1 - P_b u)C_{nc}(b)\}$$

Rearranging yields $C_{nc}(b)$ in terms of $C_{nc}(g)$:

$$(2) \qquad C_{nc}(b) = \frac{k + \beta P_b u C_{nc}(g)}{[1 - (1 - P_b u)\beta]}$$

We will use (1) and (2) above as a pair of equations in two unknowns to solve for $C_{nc}(b)$ and $C_{nc}(g)$ independent of the other.

Substituting (2) into (1) yields

$$C_{nc}(g) = \frac{P_g[F_g + \beta\left\{\dfrac{k + \beta P_b u C_{nc}(g)}{[1 - (1 - P_b u)\beta]}\right\}]}{[1 - (1 - P_g)\beta]}$$

Simplifying a great deal of algebra yields $C_{nc}(g)$ as a function of only the parameters in the model:

$$C_{nc}(g) = \frac{kP_g\beta + P_g F_g[1 - \beta + P_b u\beta]}{(1 - \beta)[1 - \beta + \beta P_b u + P_g\beta]}$$

With the exception of k, these are all given. Plugging in their values yields a final expression for $C_{nc}(g)$:

$$C_{nc}(g) = 2.17k + 39.16$$

A similar set of steps yields $C_{nc}(b)$. Substituting (1) into (2) gives

$$C_{nc}(b) = \frac{k + \beta P_b u\left\{\dfrac{P_g[F_g + \beta C_{nc}(b)]}{[1 - (1 - P_g)\beta]}\right\}}{[1 - (1 - P_b u)\beta]}$$

Simplifying this expression leads to

$$C_{nc}(b) = \frac{k[1 - (1 - P_g)\beta] + \beta P_b u P_g F_g}{(1 - \beta)[1 - \beta + \beta P_b u + P_g\beta]}$$

Substituting the given parameter values yields

$$C_{nc}(b) = 4.58k + 27.11$$

We now have 8 expressions for discounted expected costs as functions only of k. The table below summarizes the payoffs to the different strategies (the C's) conditional on initial status (b and g):

		Initial Status	
		Gold Star (g)	Black Mark (b)
Strategy	cc	$10k$	$10k$
	nn	263.16	500
	nc	$39.16 + 2.17k$	$27.11 + 4.58k$
	cn	$10k$	500

Notice that we can rule out cn as a likely strategy at this point:

If $k > 50$, nn dominates cn.

If $k \leq 50$, cc dominates cn.

$\therefore$ cn is never the "best" strategy.

The greatest value of k for which cc is always the best strategy is found by solving the following inequalities:

$10k \leq 39.16 + 2.17k$

$10k \leq 27.11 + 4.58k$

Each of these inequalities holds where $k \leq 5$

And the lowest value of k for which nn is the best strategy:

$263.16 \leq 39.16 + 2.17k$

$500 \leq 27.11 + 4.58k$

Each of these inequalities holds where $k \geq 103.2$

To summarize,

$k \leq 5 \longrightarrow cc$ is best strategy

$5 < k < 103.2 \longrightarrow nc$ is best strategy

$k \geq 103.2 \longrightarrow nn$ is best strategy.

While the exact numbers above are functions of the current example, the results here are intuitive. When compliance costs are very low (here $k < 5$), it is best for the firm to simply comply each period and avoid the risk of any fines. When compliance costs are sufficiently high (here $k > 103$), it is optimal for the firm to *never* comply, but rather face the risk of fines. When compliance costs are intermediate (here between 5 and 103), a mixed strategy of compliance only when tagged with black mark is optimal.

Chapter 17 Solutions

1. We may reasonably assume that the firm is a cost minimizer and will choose to undertake the voluntary program if the costs are lower than the expected cost of not undertaking it. If the voluntary program costs are lower then we would have reason to think that the firm would accept the voluntary program and thus it would be implementable.

Voluntary Program			*Mandatory Program*		
$TC_v(a=80)$	$=$	$10(80)$	$\mathbb{E}[TC_m(a=80)]$	$=$	$\frac{1}{2}\cdot[20(80)]$
	$=$	800		$=$	800

Since it appears that the costs are the same, and doubting that the firm is risk-loving, we can conclude that the voluntary program is implementable.

To determine the efficiency benefits to society from the voluntary program we compare the net benefits that result with (a) the net benefits from no environmental protection, and (b) the net benefits from successful mandatory regulation. From the results below we see that the voluntary program is indeed the most efficient of the three outcomes.

Voluntary Program

$$\begin{aligned}\text{Net Benefit}_v &= [TB(a=80)] - [TC_v(a=80)]\\ &= [100(80) - \tfrac{1}{2}80^2] - [10(80)]\\ &= 4000\end{aligned}$$

No Environmental Protection

$$\begin{aligned}\text{Net Benefit}_{np} &= [TB(a=0)]\\ &= [100(0) - \tfrac{1}{2}0^2]\\ &= 0\end{aligned}$$

Successful Mandatory Program

$$\begin{aligned}\text{Net Benefit}_{sm} &= [TB(a=80)] - [TC_m(a=80)]\\ &= [100(80) - \tfrac{1}{2}80^2] - [20(80)]\\ &= 3200\end{aligned}$$

2. Using the assumption that the demand curve for Finch's Frisbees (green label) is linear we derive the inverse demand curve from the information given in the question. The inverse demand curve is $P_{\text{eco}} = 2 - 1 \times 10^6 \cdot Q_{\text{eco}}$

Since we are told that Finch's competitors are sufficiently backwards we know that Tucker will hold a monopoly over the green label dog toy market. Finch's marginal revenue function, given the demand curve, will be $\text{MR}_{FF} = 2 - 2 \times 10^6 \cdot Q_{\text{eco}}$

Being told that Finch just broke even when the price of toys was \$1, we shall further assume that the marginal cost of producing dog toys is \$1 (even when they are eco-toys). Finch can now produce toys at the point where marginal revenue equals marginal cost, and thus maximize profits. The profit garnered from the production and sale of these eco-toys is the most that Finch would be willing to pay to green the company, and is \$250,000.

$$\begin{aligned} \text{MR} &\overset{set}{=} \text{MC} \\ 2 - 2 \times 10^6 \cdot Q_{\text{eco}} &= 1 \\ \Rightarrow Q^*_{\text{eco}} &= 500,000 \\ \Rightarrow P_{\text{eco}|Q=500,000} &= \$1.50 \end{aligned}$$

$$\begin{aligned} \pi_{FF} &= \text{TR}(Q^*_{\text{eco}}) - \text{TC}(Q^*_{\text{eco}}) \\ &= \$1.50(500,000) - \$1(500,000) \\ &= \$250,000 \end{aligned}$$

Chapter 18 Solutions

1. We are told that if there is a leak, then 100 additional lives will be lost. Therefore we can understand the information given in the following way:

$$\begin{aligned} P(100 \text{ deaths}|\text{no liner}) &= 0.001 \\ \Rightarrow \mathbb{E}\big[\text{number of deaths}|\text{no liner}\big] &= 0.001 \times 100 = 0.1 \text{ deaths} \end{aligned}$$

$$\begin{aligned} P(100 \text{ deaths}|\text{liner}) &= 0.0001 \\ \Rightarrow \mathbb{E}\big[\text{number of deaths}|\text{liner}\big] &= 0.0001 \times 100 = 0.01 \text{ deaths} \end{aligned}$$

We see that paying the $R1$million we save (0.1 - 0.001) = 0.09 lives over not installing the liner. Therefore if the value of fatal cancer for one life is worth more than $\frac{1\times10^6}{0.09} \approx R11.1$million then we would be justified in recomending the installation of the liner.

---

2. It seems reasonable to presume that caution will be exercised by most people in crossing the street either way: No one wants to get run over by a car! But this may provide a good metaphor for precaution in preventing theft, fire damage, and automobile accidents.

   Strict liability (without a defense of contributory negligence) would require the party responsible to pay damages to the victim regardless of the extent to which the victim took precaution to avoid the accident, i.e., in the extreme event that a pedestrian was hit by a vehicle while wandering across a busy street after intentionally blindfolding them self, the the driver would pay all damages.

   Negligence, on the other hand, would require the party responsible to pay damages only if it is shown that they failed to exercise due caution and specific actions to avoid the accident. If liability depends on negligence, someone injured while crossing the street blindfolded may not receive compensation. Being hit by a car is generally an unhappy event for a pedestrian, and its likelihood is meant to encourage pedestrians to take precautions to avoid accidents. This logic is often used to argue for liability laws based on negligence to reduce moral hazard problems.

---

3. In making decisions regarding precaution to prevent accidents, a firm considers the cost of precaution, the probabilities of an accident under different sets of precautions, the probability of being found liable for an accident, and the size of the penalty if found liable. Specifically, a firm would take more precaution the greater the probability of being found liable, and the greater the size of the penalty. It may be reasoned by the courts that some justified lawsuits are never filed, and therefore the probability the firm *perceives* of being found liable for an accident is less than the probability of *actually* being liable. To compensate for this incomplete signal to firms, the potential penalty is raised. For instance, if only 50% of victims file law suits they would win, a penalty of double damages would restore the expected penalty to the firm to the level of damages from an accident for which it is at fault.

---

4. We will assume that BP is a cost minimizer (a necessary condition for being a profit maximizing firm). By finding the cost minimizing point on BP's total cost function we can determine the thickness of the hull of their new super-tanker.

$$
\begin{aligned}
\mathrm{TC}_{\mathrm{BP}} &= P(\text{spill}) \cdot P(\text{liable}) \cdot \mathbb{E}\big[\text{damages}\big] + C(t) \\
&= (\tfrac{0.002}{t}) \cdot (0.9) \cdot \big[1 \times 10^{9}\big] + t^{2} \\
&= 14.4 \times 10^{6} t^{-1} + t^{2} \\
\Rightarrow \mathrm{MC}_{\mathrm{BP}} &= \tfrac{-14.4 \times 10^{6}}{t^{2}} + 2t \\
\tfrac{-14.4 \times 10^{6}}{t^{2}} + 2t &\stackrel{set}{=} 0 \\
\Rightarrow t^{*}_{\mathrm{BP}} &= 193.01\ cm
\end{aligned}
$$

We find the socially responsible thickness of the hull by the same calculation except we remove the probability that BP will be found liable for damages.

$$
\begin{aligned}
\mathrm{TC}_{\mathrm{soc}} &= P(\text{spill}) \cdot \mathbb{E}\big[\text{damages}\big] + C(t) \\
&= (\tfrac{0.002}{t}) \cdot \big[1 \times 10^{9}\big] + t^{2} \\
&= 16 \times 10^{6} t^{-1} + t^{2} \\
\Rightarrow \mathrm{MC}_{\mathrm{soc}} &= \tfrac{-16 \times 10^{6}}{t^{2}} + 2t \\
\tfrac{-16 \times 10^{6}}{t^{2}} + 2t &\stackrel{set}{=} 0 \\
\Rightarrow t^{*}_{\mathrm{soc}} &= 200\ cm
\end{aligned}
$$

---

5. It is difficult for insurance companies to provide coverage to companies for this type of risk due to deficiencies in at least three of the conditions for insurability outlined in the text:

   First, there is a clear moral hazard problem. The risk involved is a direct function of precaution and effort to avoid spills and evaporation, and the insurance company would want any contract to reflect these factors. The moral hazard problem arises due to the combination of two things:

   i. It is difficult for the insurance company to observe the dry cleaner's behavior in terms of precaution and effort to avoid spills.

   ii. Coverage has a negative incentive effect on precaution and effort to avoid spills.

   The extent to which the insurance company can monitor effort or require and enforce specific precautions will determine the feasibility of coverage. Removing the moral hazard problem requires either repairing the incentives for efficient precaution when covered, or allowing the insurer to observe and enforce precautionary behavior.

   Second, it may not always be possible to identify a clear loss. The dry cleaner is concerned that they may be held accountable for damages from spills and evaporation of their chemicals, but it would be difficult to anticipate what form the loss may take.

It is necessary to do so in writing insurance contracts. The problem is the ambiguity regarding what the dry cleaner will and will not be responsible for.

Third, potential losses are not restricted to a well-defined period. As discussed in the text, hazardous wastes such as chemicals from the dry cleaning process may take years to leak into the water table and years again for health effects to arise. Premiums for potential losses far in the future are likely to be prohibitively high.

---

6. Consider the scenario depicted in the figure below. The locus of points derived from Eq. (18.5) in the text is the same, as is the *slope* of the line defined Eq. (18.6), which satisfies the requirement that the probabilities of the states occurring remain the same. The problem asks to construct an example in which the expected surplus (ES) is greater than the option price (OP), leading to a negative option value (OV). This can be done by changing the state-contingent value of the risk reducing investment, described by the point (V_L, V_S) at the intersection of the Eq. (18.6) line and the Eq. (18.5) locus. (In the text, the investment is construction of a municipal water treatment plant; the value of that investment depends on whether there is a toxic leak into the city's groundwater.) In the figure below, this point is shifted up on the locus far enough that ES has become greater than OP.

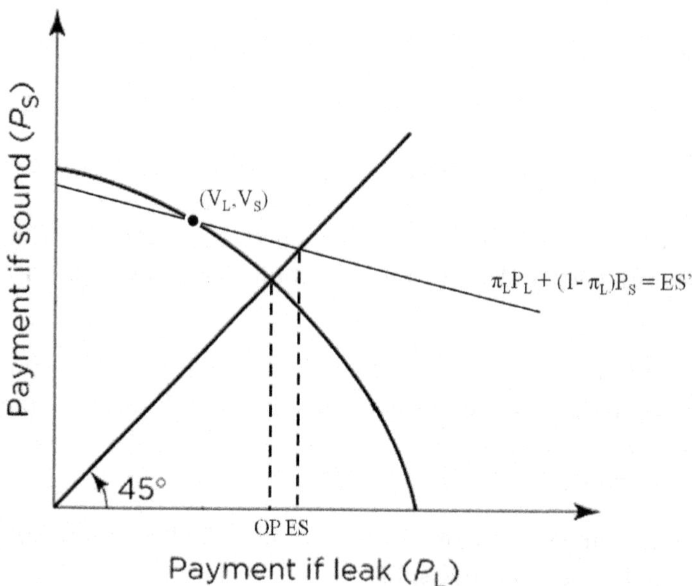

There is a logical contradiction in drawing this scenario as it is in the figure above. A necessary condition for $ES > OP$ with the current probabilities is that the point describing the state-contingent value of the investment be above the 45° line. That is, generating the outcome requested in the problem requires $V_S > V_L$, meaning that the water treatment plant would be *more valuable* if there was no leak into the groundwater. This is very counterintuitive: investments to reduce risk are undertaken because they have a payoff in the event of a bad outcome. If the payoff is greater when nothing bad happens, the investment really does not qualify as risk-reducing, and the example does not apply.

7. See the figure below for a graphical representation of the problem. Added to Figure 18.3 in the text are lines with the same slope as the line described by Eq. (18.6), labeled L, L', L''. These are the "loan lines" and represent combinations of state-contingent payments whose expected value is equal to some fixed value. That fixed value in this context is the amount of the loan.

   The statement in the question that "[t]he expected value of the payments is equal to the amount loaned" defines a line for a loan of value L :

   $\pi_L P_L + (1 - \pi_L)Ps = L$

   This line has a slope of $-\frac{\pi_L}{1-\pi_L}$, same as the line defined by Eq. (18.6) in the text. For $L' > L$, the line defined by $\pi_L P_L + (1 - \pi_L)Ps = L'$ lies above line L with the same slope. Recall that the concave curve from Eq. (18.5) represents combinations of state-contingent prices that are equivalent in utility to not financing the water project at all. It is, in this sense, a willingness-to-pay frontier.

   The highest loan amount is line L', which is tangent to the curve at point A. Point A is a combination of state-contingent payments which this community is *just willing* to pay in order to finance the water project. The expected value of these payments is L'. No loan amount larger than L' shares any points with this frontier, and therefore could not be financed in this way (e.g., line L''). The amount loaned is independent of the state (paid before the state is revealed), so is interpretable as the (equal) state contingent payments at the point where L' intersects the 45° line. This is the so-called "fair bet point," labeled FBP.

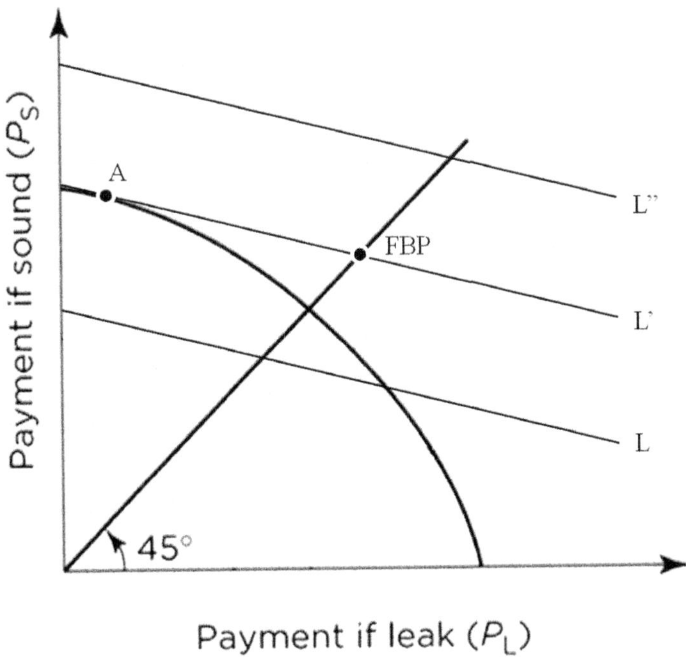

8. a. The expected value of the benefits is $\$1.08 \times 10^9$, the net benefit of building the dam today is $\$0.08 \times 10^9$.

   Net Benefit $= 0.9(1.2 \times 10^9 - 1.0 \times 10^9) + 0.1(0 - 1.0 \times 10^9) = \$0.08 \times 10^9$

   b. The net benefit today of deferring the decision one year and knowing with certainty the the project is needed or not results in an discounted net benefit of $\$0.171 \times 10^9$.

   Net Benefit $= \frac{1}{1.05}\left[0.9)(1.2 \times 10^9 - 1.0 \times 10^9) + 0.1(0)\right] = \$0.171 \times 10^9$

Chapter 19 Solutions

1. We have a subsidy to the firm in D, chosen by the government in D, but no subsidy in F. From the equations in the text, the profits for the two countries:

   $$\Pi_D = [a - b(D+F)]D + sD - C_D = (a + s - bF)D - bD^2 - C_D$$

   $$\Pi_F = [a - b(D+F)]F - C_F = (a - bD)F - bF^2 - C_F$$

   Each firm in each country maximizes profit, assuming output in the other country is fixed:

   $$\frac{d\Pi_D}{dD} = a + s - bF - 2bD = 0$$

   $$D = \frac{(a + s - bF)}{2b} \qquad (D\text{'s reaction function})$$

   $$\frac{d\Pi_F}{dF} = a - bD - 2bF = 0$$

   $$F = \frac{(a - bD)}{2b} \qquad (F\text{'s reaction function})$$

   The Cournot equilibrium is found where these reaction functions cross. Solve for the equilibrium values by substituting one reaction function into the other:

   $$D = \frac{a + s - b[\frac{a-bD}{2b}]}{2b} = \frac{a + s - \frac{a}{2} + \frac{bD}{2}}{2b}$$

   $$D(2b - \tfrac{b}{2}) = \tfrac{a}{2} + s$$

   $$D^* = \frac{\frac{a}{2} + s}{\frac{3}{2}b} = \frac{(a+2s)}{3b}$$

   $$F = \frac{a - b[\frac{a+s-bF}{2b}]}{2b} = \frac{a - \frac{a}{2} - \frac{s}{2} + \frac{bF}{2}}{2b}$$

   $$F(2b - \tfrac{b}{2}) = \tfrac{a}{2} - \tfrac{s}{2}$$

   $$F^* = \frac{\frac{a}{2} - \frac{s}{2}}{\frac{3}{2}b} = \frac{(a-s)}{3b}$$

   F^* and D^* represent the equilibrium outputs for the foreign and domestic firms, respectively, as functions of $a, b,$ and s. The domestic government wants to choose s to maximize net profit ($D's$ profit minus the subsidy). We know that this will be

   $$\Pi_D - sD^* = [a - b(F^* + D^*)]D^* - C_D$$

   Plugging in the values found above for F^* and D^*, we obtain

   $$\text{Net profit} = [a - b(\tfrac{a-s}{3b})](\tfrac{a+2s}{3b}) - b(\tfrac{a+2s}{3b})^2 - C_D$$

   Simplifying this expression yields

   $$\text{NP} = \left(\frac{2a}{3} + \frac{s}{3}\right) \cdot \left(\frac{a+2s}{3b}\right) - \frac{(a+2s)^2}{9b} - C_D$$

The domestic government wants to choose s to maximize this quantity:

$$\frac{d\text{NP}}{ds} = \frac{1}{3}\left(\frac{a+2s}{3b}\right) + \frac{2}{3b}\left(\frac{2a+s}{3}\right) - \frac{4(a+2s)}{9b} = 0$$

Multiply through this expression by $9b$:

$a + 2s + 4a + 2s - 4a - 8s = 0$

$4s = a$

$s^* = \frac{a}{4}$

So the optimal subsidy will be positive and depend only on the parameter a.

---

2. The statement is valid. The empirical evidence related to the relationship between income and environmental quality, the "environmental Kuznets curve," is derived from cross-sectional data. It is not clear that inverted-U relationships, when they are found, should apply to time series of those variables for the same country. There are a number of reasons to say this, and one of them is demonstrated in Figure 19.2 in the text.

   The figure reveals that the cross-sectional paths are changing over time. This is perhaps due to innovation and diffusion of technology; for safe drinking water, the diffusion of knowledge regarding what makes people sick and innovation in chemical treatment are examples. The paths of these variables, therefore, are almost surely going to be different for countries that develop in different historical periods. For this example, this is good news: countries currently reaching middle income appear likely to reach near-universal safe drinking water faster (at lower per capita income) than currently developed countries.

---

3. The Samuelson condition for the optimal provision of a public good is:

$$\sum_{i=1}^{L} \text{MRS} = \text{MRT}$$

   Because the good (or bad) is nonrival, the *sum* of the marginal rates of substitution must be equal to the marginal rate of transformation. But the indifference curve in the figure is tangent to the MRT, suggesting $\text{MRS}_i = \text{MRT}$.

   The frontier BD in Figure 19.6 is in the text the set of attainable combinations of c and E, where c is per capita consumption in the community. If c represents consumption of the representative consumer, then

$$\text{MRS} = \frac{dc}{dE} = -\frac{u'_E}{u'_C}.$$

   The Samuelson condition would require then that

$$\text{MRT} = -\frac{u'_E}{u'_C} \cdot \overline{L}.$$

This is in fact the case here because the slope of the frontier BD is not the MRT, since total consumption is $c\overline{L}$. The slope of this line is $\frac{\text{MRT}}{\overline{L}}$. At the point of tangency, the MRS $= \frac{\text{MRT}}{\overline{L}}$. Summing over the $\overline{L}$ identical individuals satisfies the condition.

---

4. We begin by deriving each firms reaction function from their respective profit functions. Since the firms in each country are identical, their profit and thus their reaction functions will be symmetrical.

$$\begin{aligned}\pi_D &= \text{TR}_D - \text{TC}_D\\ &= P \cdot Q_D - C(Q_D)\\ &= (10 - Q_D - Q_F) \cdot Q_D - 1 \text{ from the text } VC(Q_D) = 0, \text{ from the question } FC = 1\\ &= 10Q_D - Q_D^2 - Q_F Q_D - 1\end{aligned}$$

$$\begin{aligned}\frac{\partial \pi_D}{\partial Q_D} &= 10 - 2Q_D - Q_F \quad \stackrel{set}{=} 0\\ \Rightarrow Q_D' &= 5 - \tfrac{1}{2}Q_F \quad \text{the domestic firm's profit maximizing reaction function}\\ Q_F' &= 5 - \tfrac{1}{2}Q_D \quad \text{the foreign firm's profit maximizing reaction function}\end{aligned}$$

a. The plot of the domestic firm's and the foreign firm's best response functions are shown in the figure below. Also shown are several iso-profit lines for the domestic firm.

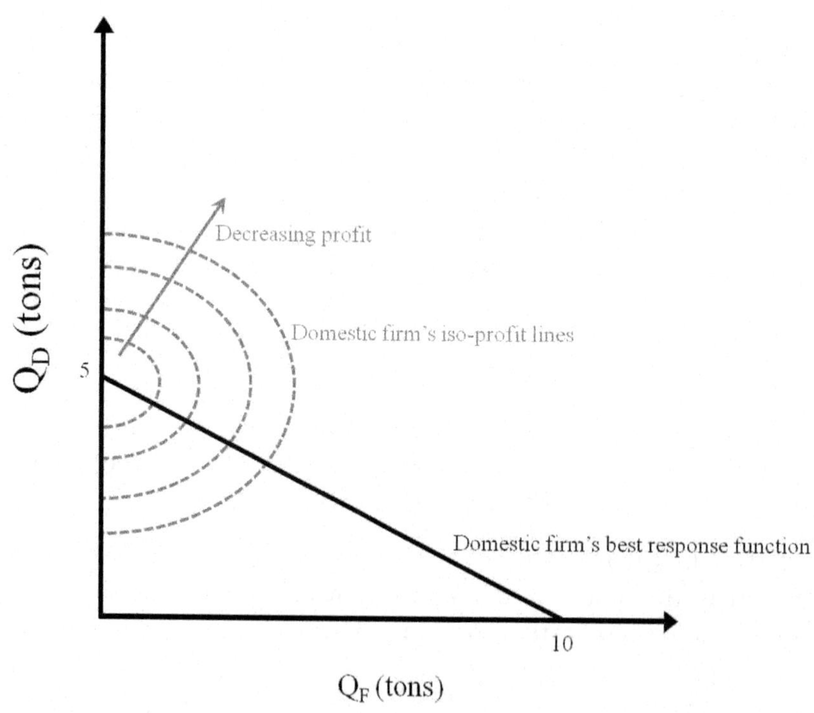

b. The figure below shows the foreign firm's best response function as well as the domestic firm's function. The intersection is the Cournot equilibrium, the levels of output associated with this equilibrium are calculated below. The profit for each firm and each country are also calculated below.

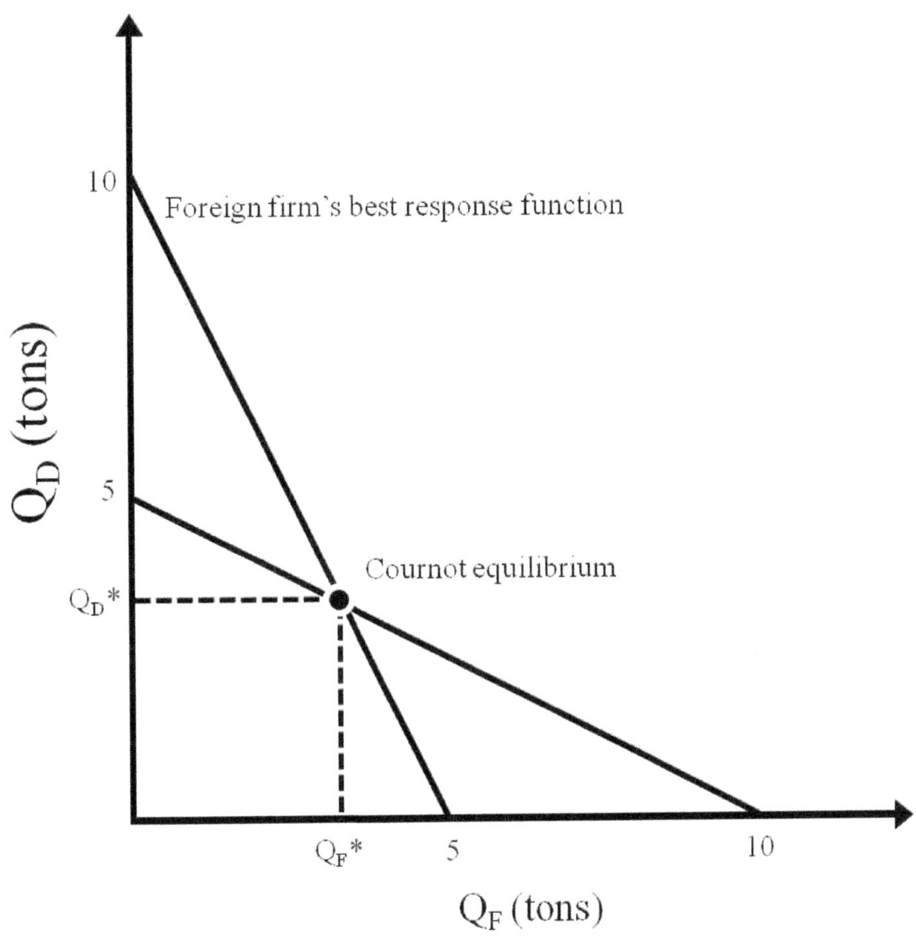

$$
\begin{aligned}
5 - \tfrac{1}{2}Q_F &= 10 - 2Q_F \qquad \text{solving one reaction function for the other} \\
1\tfrac{1}{2}Q_F &= 5 \\
\Rightarrow Q_F^* &= 3\tfrac{1}{3} \\
\Rightarrow Q_D^* &= 3\tfrac{1}{3}
\end{aligned}
$$

$$
\begin{aligned}
\pi_D &= 10Q_D - Q_D^2 - Q_F Q_D - 1 \\
&= 10(3\tfrac{1}{3}) - (3\tfrac{1}{3})^2 - (3\tfrac{1}{3})(3\tfrac{1}{3}) - 1 \\
&= 10\tfrac{1}{9} \\
\Rightarrow \pi_F &= 10\tfrac{1}{9}
\end{aligned}
$$

Since there are no subsidies then each country's profit is the same as their respective firm's profit.

c. We derive the domestic firm's profit function anew to include the domestic country \$0.50 subsidy, then plot the functions in the figure below.

$$\begin{aligned}
\pi_{D|s_D=0.5} &= \text{TR}_D - \text{TC}_D \\
&= P \cdot Q_D + s \cdot Q_D - C(Q_D) \\
&= (10 - Q_D - Q_F) \cdot Q_D + \tfrac{1}{2} Q_D - 1 \\
&= 10\tfrac{1}{2} Q_D - Q_D^2 - Q_F Q_D - 1
\end{aligned}$$

$$\begin{aligned}
\frac{\partial \pi_D}{\partial Q_D} &= 10\tfrac{1}{2} - 2Q_D - Q_F \overset{set}{=} 0 \\
\Rightarrow Q'_{D|s_D=0.5} &= 5\tfrac{1}{4} - \tfrac{1}{2} Q_F \quad \text{the domestic firm's reaction function} \\
Q'_F &= 5 - \tfrac{1}{2} Q_D \quad \text{the foreign firm's reaction function is unchanged}
\end{aligned}$$

$$\begin{aligned}
5\tfrac{1}{4} - \tfrac{1}{2} Q_F &= 10 - 2Q_F \quad \text{solving one reaction function for the other} \\
1\tfrac{1}{2} Q_F &= 4\tfrac{3}{4} \\
\Rightarrow Q_F^* &= 3\tfrac{1}{6} \\
\Rightarrow Q_D^* &= 3\tfrac{2}{3}
\end{aligned}$$

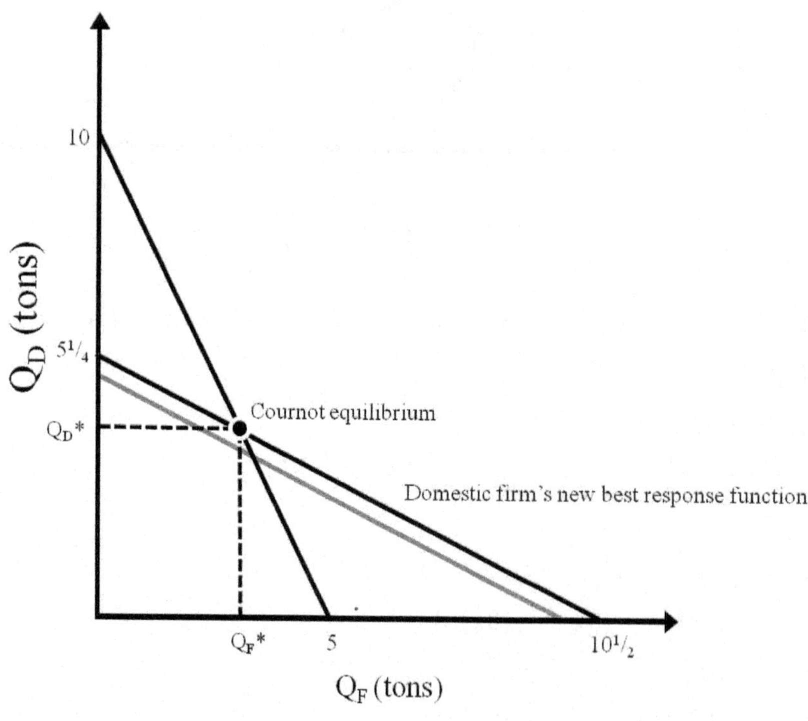

d. The profit for the domestic firm is \$12.44 and the profit for the foreign firm is \$9.03 The profit for the domestic country is the domestic firm's profit minus the subsidy and is \$10.61, while the profit for the foreign country is the same as the foreign firm's profit of \$9.03. The domestic country has clearly done better by subsidizing the domestic firm, compared to when neither country provided a subsidy in part (b).

$$\begin{aligned}\pi_{D|s_D=0.5} &= 10\tfrac{1}{2}Q_D - Q_D^2 - Q_F Q_D - 1\\ &= 10\tfrac{1}{2}(3\tfrac{2}{3}) - (3\tfrac{2}{3})^2 - (3\tfrac{1}{6})(3\tfrac{2}{3}) - 1\\ &= 12\tfrac{4}{9}\end{aligned}$$

$$\begin{aligned}\pi_{F|s_D=0.5} &= 10Q_F - Q_F^2 - Q_D Q_F - 1\\ &= 10(3\tfrac{1}{6}) - (3\tfrac{1}{6})^2 - (3\tfrac{2}{3})(3\tfrac{1}{6}) - 1\\ &= 9\tfrac{1}{36}\end{aligned}$$

e. The reaction functions for each country is stated below along with a plot of the new reaction functions in the figure below. By running through the same calculations above with the new reaction functions, we find that $Q^*_{D|s_D=0.5,s_F=0.5} = 3\frac{1}{2}$, and $Q^*_{F|s_D=0.5,s_F=0.5} = 3\frac{1}{2}$

$$Q'_{D|s_D=0.5,s_F=0.5} = 5\tfrac{1}{4} - \tfrac{1}{2}Q_F \qquad \text{the domestic firm's new reaction function}$$

$$Q'_{F|s_D=0.5,s_F=0.5} = 5\tfrac{1}{4} - \tfrac{1}{2}Q_D \qquad \text{the foreign firm's new reaction function}$$

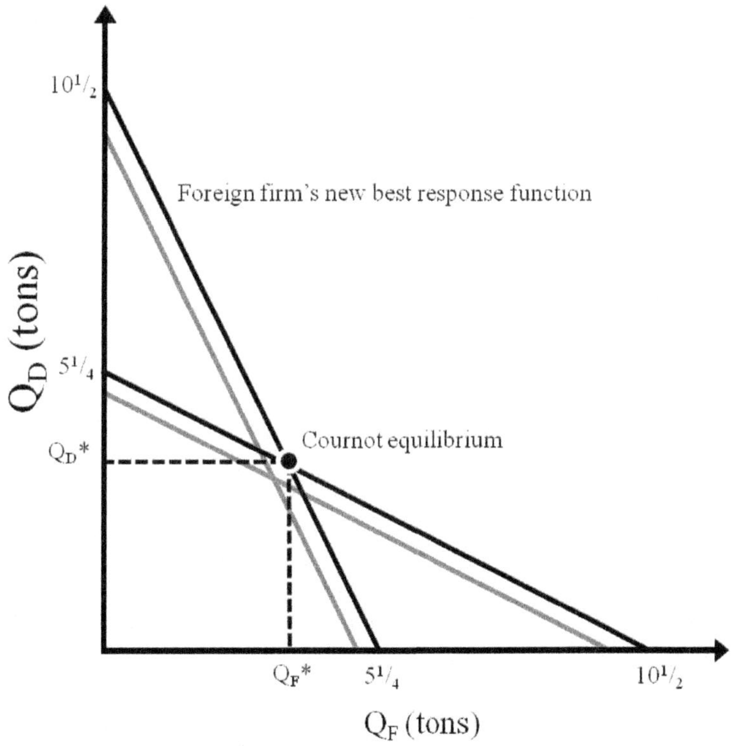

f. We calculate each firms profit similarly as above and find $\pi_{F|s_D=0.5,s_F=0.5} = \$11.25$ for both firms, and the profit to each country is the their firm's profit minus the subsidy and is \$9.50. Compared to part (b) we see that although both firm's profits have increased it comes at a cost to each country. In fact the total surplus is \$1 less than when there were no subsidies.

5. Apparently a memo signed by Lawrence Summers, the then chief economist of the World Bank, purported three reasons for considering the encouragement of more hazardous waste exports to developing countries. First, that the measurement of the health effects on lost earnings due to hazardous waste exposure would be lower in low income countries. Second, that the underpopulated developing countries are underpolluted relative to more densely populated developed countries. Third, that demand for environmental quality in developing countries is likely to be very income elastic. The memo purported that these things imply that encouraging the export of hazardous waste to developing countries could be welfare enhancing.

   Arguments against this position generally center around the exploitation of very low income people in developing countries. Many people may feel a sense of environmental injustice about exporting hazardous wastes to countries where labor and environmental laws may be less stringent or even nonexistent. Such perspectives prompted Michael Prowse to write an article entitled "Save Planet Earth from Economists" in the *Financial Times*, February 10, 1992.

Chapter 20 Solutions

1. We can use Eq. (20.7) from the text to measure the labor factor productivity growth, and we can use Eq. (20.6) from the text to calculate total factor productivity growth from the data given (using 1997 as the base). To calculate the total factor productivity growth including pollution we will adjust Eq. (20.7) to include pollution as an input just as capital is included:

$$\begin{aligned}
\text{Labor productivity growth} &= \frac{\dot{Y}}{Y} - \frac{\dot{L}}{L} \\
&= \frac{Y_{1998} - Y_{1997}}{Y_{1997}} - \frac{L_{1998} - L_{1997}}{L_{1997}} \\
&= \frac{3{,}000}{100{,}000} - \frac{1}{50} \\
&= 0.01
\end{aligned}$$

$$\begin{aligned}
\text{Total productivity growth} &= \frac{\dot{Y}}{Y} - s_L\frac{\dot{L}}{L} - s_K\frac{\dot{K}}{K} \\
&= \frac{\dot{Y}}{Y} - \frac{p_L L}{(p_L L + p_K K)} \cdot \frac{\dot{L}}{L} - \frac{p_K K}{(p_L L + p_K K)} \cdot \frac{\dot{K}}{K} \\
&= \frac{3 \times 10^3}{100 \times 10^3} - \frac{5 \times 10^5}{7 \times 10^5} \cdot \frac{1}{50} - \frac{2 \times 10^5}{7 \times 10^5} \cdot \frac{0}{1 \times 10^6} \\
&= 0.16
\end{aligned}$$

$$\begin{aligned}
\text{Total productivity growth (pollution)} &= \frac{\dot{Y}}{Y} - s_L\frac{\dot{L}}{L} - s_K\frac{\dot{K}}{K} - s_P\frac{\dot{P}}{P} \\
&= \frac{\dot{Y}}{Y} - \frac{p_L L}{(p_L L + p_K K + p_P P)} \cdot \frac{\dot{L}}{L} - 0 - \frac{p_P P}{(p_L L + p_K K + p_P P)} \cdot \frac{\dot{P}}{P} \\
&= \frac{3 \times 10^3}{100 \times 10^3} - \frac{5 \times 10^5}{9 \times 10^5} \cdot \frac{1}{50} - \frac{2 \times 10^5}{9 \times 10^5} \cdot \frac{-10}{20} \\
&= 0.13
\end{aligned}$$

---

2. If there were no land reclamation law requiring AJAX to pay £10,000, then although the company would save on that cost, the damage, so we are told, would be £20,000. Thus when we account net domestic product (including natural resource depletion and land degradation) it would be reduced to £240,000.

   The difference reflects the fact that had the reclamation efforts been undertaken, then the value of the damage avoided would have been £20,000, but it would have only cost £10,000.

---

3. The statement is valid. The empirical evidence related to the relationship between income and environmental quality, the "environmental Kuznets curve," is derived from cross-sectional data. It is not at all clear that inverted-U relationships, when they are found, should apply to time series of those variables for the same country. There are a number of reasons to say this, and one of them is demonstrated in Figure 19.2 in the text.

   The figure reveals that the cross-sectional paths are changing over time. This is perhaps due to innovation and diffusion of technology; for safe drinking water, the diffusion of knowledge regarding what makes people sick and innovation in chemical treatment are examples. The paths of these variables, therefore, are almost surely going to be different for countries that develop in different historical periods. For this example, this is good news: countries currently reaching middle income appear likely to reach near-universal safe drinking water faster (at lower per capita income) than currently developed countries.

CPSIA information can be obtained
at www.ICGtesting.com
Printed in the USA
BVOW11s1136210118
505516BV00009B/195/P